Pickling and Fermenting Recipes for Survival

Delicious Dishes for the Long Haul

Ethan Roberts

Table of Contents

INTRODUCTION

The traditional methods of pickling and fermenting provide priceless answers in a world where food security is a critical issue and self-sufficiency is becoming increasingly appreciated. "Pickling and Fermenting Recipes for Survival: Delicious Dishes for the Long Haul" explores the science and art of food preservation using these time-tested methods, offering a thorough manual for anyone looking for ways to preserve food and guarantee survival during uncertain times.

Resilient food preservation methods are more important than ever as we traverse a time of economic instability, environmental volatility, and global health concerns. With a long history dating back to humankind, pickling and fermenting provide a technique to preserve perishable foods while also opening doors to savory and nourishing foods that are not limited by seasonality.

The first few chapters of this book take us on a voyage of exploration as we go over the foundations of pickling and fermenting. Readers will have a comprehensive grasp of the methods that constitute the foundation of long-term food preservation, from the fundamental ideas behind each procedure to the necessary tools for success. Additionally, we explore the wide range of components—from colorful veggies to aromatic spices—that function as the foundation for pickled and fermented goods.

"Pickling and Fermenting Recipes for Survival" is primarily a compilation of recipes that have been carefully chosen to accommodate a wide range of palates. There is something in these pages that will please every palette, whether it is the nuanced umami flavors of kimchi, the fiery sting of fermented hot sauce, or the tangy crunch of pickled cucumbers. Even inexperienced fermenters can confidently take on gastronomic adventures due to the comprehensive directions and valuable advice provided, and experienced practitioners will find motivation to expand their creative horizons.

Pickling and fermenting provide a route to resiliency, empowerment, and connection—to our food, our communities, and the age-old wisdom of our ancestors—beyond simple nutrition. May "Pickling and Fermenting Recipes for Survival" be a source of inspiration and strength for you as we set out on this adventure together, pointing readers toward a time when prosperity and independence coexist.

CHAPTER I

Pickling and Fermenting Overview

Importance of pickling and fermenting for survival

The importance of pickling and fermenting for survival stretches back thousands of years and spans across nearly every culture around the globe. These processes represent culinary tradition and signify a profound understanding of food preservation that has played a crucial role in human survival. The techniques of pickling and fermenting have allowed societies to extend the shelf life of perishable foods, enhancing food security through the seasons and in times of scarcity. This section delves into the significance of these age-old practices, exploring their benefits, historical context, and their continued relevance in modern times.

Pickling, the process of preserving food by immersion in vinegar or brine, and fermenting, the conversion of carbohydrates to alcohol or organic acids employing microorganisms, are both methods designed to inhibit the growth of food-spoiling bacteria. Historically, these processes were developed out of necessity, as early humans sought ways to store surplus food safely. Before the advent of refrigeration and chemical preservatives, these were among the few methods available to prevent food spoilage and ensure a steady food supply throughout the year. By enabling the preservation of fruits, vegetables, meats, and fish, pickling and fermenting played a pivotal role in human survival and the development of civilization.

The importance of these processes extends beyond mere preservation. Fermentation, in particular, enhances the nutritional value of food. It introduces beneficial bacteria, or probiotics, into the diet, which are crucial for maintaining gut health and strengthening the immune system. Foods such as yogurt, kimchi, and sauerkraut are not only preserved through fermentation but are also enriched with vitamins and minerals. The fermentation process can increase the availability of certain nutrients, making the food more nutritious than its raw counterpart. Moreover, pickling and fermenting can break down substances that may be difficult to digest, making these foods more accessible to a broader array of people.

Historically, the significance of pickling and fermenting can be observed in numerous ancient civilizations. The ancient Egyptians, for instance, fermented grains to make beer and used similar techniques to preserve vegetables and fish. In Asia, fermentation has been a cornerstone of culinary tradition, with soy sauce, kimchi, and various pickled vegetables playing essential roles in the diet. Similarly, in Europe, sauerkraut and pickled cucumbers have been staples for centuries. These practices were culinary traditions and basic survival strategies that enabled societies to thrive in diverse environments.

In contemporary times, the relevance of pickling and fermenting continues, albeit for slightly different reasons. In an age where industrialized food production often prioritizes convenience over nutrition, these traditional methods offer a sustainable alternative. They represent a return to whole, unprocessed foods, providing a way to preserve seasonal produce without the need for artificial preservatives or refrigeration. This reduces reliance on energy-intensive storage methods and encourages a closer connection to the food we eat and its origins. Furthermore, in the context of global food security, these techniques offer practical solutions for reducing food waste and ensuring a more stable food supply.

Additionally, the revival of interest in these methods has been partly driven by growing awareness of their health benefits. As modern science uncovers more about the human microbiome and its impact on health, the value of fermented foods, mainly, has come into the spotlight. This has led to a resurgence in home fermenting and pickling, with individuals seeking to incorporate these healthful foods into their diets. It's a trend that embraces the wisdom of ancient food preservation techniques and aligns with contemporary concerns about health, sustainability, and food sovereignty.

In conclusion, the importance of pickling and fermenting for survival cannot be overstated. These methods have been instrumental in human history, enabling societies to overcome the challenges of food preservation and scarcity. They have enriched our diets, introduced vital nutrients, and offered a means to manage our food resources sustainably. As we face the challenges of the

21st century, including global food insecurity and the need for sustainable food practices, the lessons learned from pickling and fermenting remain as relevant as ever. By embracing these traditional methods, we can address some of today's most pressing issues, ensuring a healthier, more sustainable future for generations to come. Through this lens, pickling and fermenting are not just about survival but about thriving in harmony with nature and our cultural heritage.

Historical significance of pickling and fermenting

The historical significance of pickling and fermenting encompasses a fascinating journey through human civilization, revealing not just a story of culinary evolution but also of survival, culture, and innovation. These age- old techniques, which involve preserving food through anaerobic fermentation in brine or vinegar, have roots that stretch back to ancient times, influencing and being influenced by the societies that practiced them. This section explores the rich history of pickling and fermenting, shedding light on their roles in human development, cultural exchanges, and the spread of culinary traditions across the globe.

The origins of pickling and fermenting are as ancient as civilization itself, with evidence suggesting that some of the earliest human societies employed these practices. Archaeological finds, including jars of pickled vegetables in the Tigris Valley, date back to 2400 BC, indicating that ancient Mesopotamians utilized fermentation and pickling as methods of food preservation. Similarly, ancient Egyptians are known to have pickled fish and cucumbers, showcasing the widespread application of these techniques in preserving various foods. The significance of these methods was profound; they not only allowed for storing surplus food, preventing spoilage, and ensuring availability during scarce times but also facilitated long journeys and trade by providing durable food sources.

As trade routes expanded, the knowledge of pickling and fermenting spread, influencing and integrating into different cultures worldwide. The Greeks and Romans adopted these practices, with records from these civilizations highlighting the use of pickled vegetables and fermented sauces to complement their diets. The Roman legions were notably supplied with fermented cabbage, which was believed to maintain their health and stamina during extended campaigns. This practice highlights the early understanding of the health benefits associated with fermented foods, a precursor to modern probiotics.

In Asia, fermentation became a cornerstone of culinary tradition, giving rise to various fermented foods that are still integral to diets today. For example, soy sauce, derived from the fermentation of soybeans and grains, originated in China over 2,000 years ago and spread throughout Asia, becoming a staple ingredient. Korea's kimchi, a fermented vegetable dish with a history dating back to the first century AD, is another example of the deep cultural significance of fermentation. These practices were not merely about preserving food; they were an art form deeply intertwined with communities' cultural and spiritual life, marking seasons and celebrations.

The Middle Ages saw the continuation and expansion of pickling and fermenting practices throughout Europe. The scarcity of fresh food during winter months and the need for nutritious food during long sea voyages spurred innovation in these methods. Sailors, including those on the voyages of Christopher Columbus, relied on pickled and fermented foods for sustenance, demonstrating the critical role these techniques played in the exploration and expansion of the world as known at the time. The age of exploration was partly enabled by these food preservation methods, allowing explorers to travel further distances and survive in new lands.

The industrial revolution and the advent of canning and refrigeration changed the role of pickling and fermenting in society. However, rather than disappearing, these methods evolved. They shifted from being essential survival techniques to becoming means of cultural expression and health. In the 19th and 20th centuries, as industrial food production increased, traditional methods of food preservation saw a decline. Yet, in many cultures, these practices were maintained as part of culinary heritage, cherished for the unique flavors they imparted to food.

In the 21st century, interest in traditional pickling and fermenting methods has been resurgent. This revival is driven by a growing appreciation for the complex flavors these processes bring to food and an increasing awareness of their health benefits. Modern science has begun to uncover the microbiome's significance in human health, lending credence to the ancient wisdom encapsulated in fermented foods. Today, fermented foods are celebrated for their probiotic properties, contributing to a healthy digestive system and improved immunity.

Moreover, the historical significance of pickling and fermenting extends beyond nutrition and health, reflecting a deep connection to the earth and its seasons. These practices represent a sustainable food consumption and preservation approach, reducing waste by utilizing excess produce and eliminating the need for artificial preservatives. In a world grappling with the consequences of industrial food production and environmental degradation, the ancient wisdom of pickling and fermenting offers valuable lessons in sustainability and respect for nature.

In conclusion, the historical significance of pickling and fermenting is immense, encompassing themes of survival, health, cultural exchange, and sustainability. These methods have not only enabled human civilizations to thrive and expand but have also enriched our culinary traditions, offering a bridge to the past and a guide for the future. As we continue to explore and appreciate the depth of these practices, we recognize them as a testament to human ingenuity and resilience. The story of pickling and fermenting is a vivid reminder of our shared history, a unifying thread that connects us to our ancestors and to each other, across cultures and through time.

Benefits of pickling and fermenting for long-term food preservation

The benefits of pickling and fermenting for long-term food preservation are manifold, offering a means to lengthen the shelf life of foods as well as improve their nutritional value, flavor, and digestibility. These ancient practices, which date back thousands of years, have been pivotal in human survival and the advancement of civilizations. As we delve into the reasons behind the effectiveness of these methods, it becomes clear that their significance extends beyond mere preservation to include health benefits, sustainability, and culinary diversity.

Pickling involves preserving food in an acidic environment, typically created with vinegar or through the natural fermentation process that produces lactic acid. Conversely, fermenting relies on microorganisms' action to convert sugars into alcohol or acids, creating an environment that inhibits the growth of spoilage-causing bacteria. Both methods drastically slow down the decomposition process, allowing foods to be stored for months or even years without spoiling. This capacity for long-term preservation has been essential for human survival, particularly in regions with long winters or unpredictable food supplies.

One of the primary benefits of these preservation techniques is enhancing nutritional value. The fermentation process, in particular, can increase the availability of vitamins and minerals in foods, making them more nutritious than their fresh counterparts. Fermented foods are rich in probiotics, helpful bacteria that are crucial in maintaining gut health and enhancing the immune system. The consumption of fermented foods has been interconnected to enhanced digestion, better nutrient absorption, and a reduced risk of some diseases. Moreover, fermentation can break down indigestible or harmful compounds, making the food safer and easier to digest.

From a culinary perspective, pickling and fermenting introduce a variety of flavors and textures to the diet, enriching the culinary landscape with an array of tastes that cannot be achieved through fresh produce alone. These methods can transform simple ingredients into complex, flavorful foods with distinct sour, tangy, or umami tastes. The diverse range of pickled and fermented products across different cultures—from kimchi in Korea to sauerkraut in Germany, and pickled cucumbers in many parts of the world—illustrates the versatility and adaptability of these preservation techniques to local tastes and ingredients.

Sustainability is another significant benefit of pickling and fermenting. Extending the shelf life of produce can help reduce food waste, a critical issue in the modern world, where vast amounts of food are discarded annually. They enable the efficient use of seasonal surpluses, allowing for the enjoyment of fruits and vegetables throughout the year without the need for energy-intensive refrigeration or the environmental impact of transporting fresh produce over long distances. In this way, pickling and fermenting contribute to a more sustainable food system, emphasizing the use of local resources and minimizing the carbon footprint associated with food preservation.

Moreover, pickling and fermenting require no electricity, making them accessible and practical preservation methods for people living in areas without reliable access to power. This aspect underscores the relevance of these techniques in traditional settings and contemporary contexts where sustainable living and self-sufficiency are increasingly valued. The simplicity and low cost of these methods also democratize food preservation, making it possible for virtually anyone to extend the life of their food.

Despite these benefits, it's essential to acknowledge that successful pickling and fermenting require knowledge and care to ensure food safety. The proper balance of salt, acidity, and temperature is necessary to inhibit the growth of harmful bacteria while allowing beneficial microorganisms to thrive. However, with some practice and adherence to guidelines, these risks can be managed effectively, allowing individuals to enjoy the fruits of their labor safely.

In conclusion, the benefits of pickling and fermenting for long-term food preservation are extensive, encompassing nutritional enhancement, culinary diversity, sustainability, and accessibility. These time-honored techniques offer a bridge between the past and the future, providing a means to preserve food and enrich our diets, reduce waste, and foster a deeper connection with the traditions that have sustained humanity for millennia. As we face the challenges of feeding a growing global population and mitigating the environmental impact of our food systems, the ancient practices of pickling and fermenting stand out as relevant, sustainable solutions. By embracing these methods, we can tap into the wisdom of our ancestors to create a more sustainable, healthful, and flavorful future.

CHAPTER II

Understanding Pickling and Fermenting

What is pickling?

Pickling is a timeless method of food preservation that has been part of human culinary practices for thousands of years. This technique involves preserving food by anaerobic fermentation in brine or immersion in vinegar, creating an environment that inhibits the development of spoilage-causing microorganisms. The result is an extension of the food's shelf life and a transformation in its taste, texture, and nutritional properties. This section explores the intricacies of pickling, its historical origins, the science behind it, its cultural significance, and the variety it brings to the global culinary landscape.

The roots of pickling stretch back to ancient civilizations, where the necessity to preserve food for leaner times led to the development of various preservation methods. Evidence of pickling has been found in the ancient civilizations of Mesopotamia, Egypt, China, and Greece, among others. These early practices laid the groundwork for the pickling techniques we know today, demonstrating humanity's ingenuity in ensuring food security and diversifying their diets. Pickling allowed for the safe storage of surplus harvests and provided nutritious food during seasons when fresh produce was scarce or during long voyages.

At the heart of pickling is the science of preservation. The process typically involves submerging the food in a solution of water and salt (brine) or vinegar. In the case of fermentation pickles, the brine creates an anaerobic environment that promotes the development of beneficial bacteria, primarily Lactobacillus. These bacteria convert sugars in the food into lactic acid, which serves as a natural preservative. The acidic environment prevents the development of harmful microorganisms that cause food spoilage and disease. On the other hand, vinegar pickles are made by immersing food in a solution of vinegar, water, and salt, sometimes with additional sugar and spices for flavor. The high acidity of vinegar serves a similar preservative function as lactic acid, killing off or inhibiting the growth of spoilage-causing bacteria.

The cultural significance of pickling is as varied as the methods and ingredients used in different regions of the world. Each culture has developed unique pickling traditions, often deeply embedded in its culinary heritage. In Korea, kimchi, a fermented vegetable dish, is a staple in meals; in Eastern Europe, pickled cucumbers and sauerkraut are essential side dishes; in India, a wide variety of pickles made from fruits, vegetables, and even meats are consumed for their intense flavors and digestive benefits. Through the decades, these traditions have preserved not only food but also cultural identity and history.

Pickling introduces various flavors and textures to the diet, transforming ordinary ingredients into tangy, crisp, and flavorful delicacies. The process can enhance the natural taste of the food or infuse it with new flavors by adding spices, herbs, and other seasonings. This transformation not only adds variety and interest to meals but also increases the palatability and appeal of preserved foods. Moreover, pickled foods often contain probiotics, beneficial bacteria that promote gut health, showcasing the added health benefits of specific pickling methods.

In modern times, the art of pickling has experienced a resurgence in popularity among chefs, home cooks, and food enthusiasts seeking to explore traditional preservation methods and the complex flavors they offer.

This renewed interest is also driven by a growing awareness of the health advantages of fermented foods and a desire for sustainable food practices. Pickling at home has become a way to reduce food waste, extend the life of seasonal produce, and create unique, homemade flavors that can't be found in store-bought products.

Despite its simplicity, successful pickling requires knowledge and attention to detail. Factors such as the concentration of brine or vinegar, the type of salt used, the temperature, and the fermentation time all play crucial roles in the safety as well as quality of the final product. Adhering to tried-and-tested recipes and understanding the science behind the process can help ensure that home-pickled foods are not only delicious but are also safe to eat.

In conclusion, pickling is a fascinating and multifaceted culinary practice that encompasses the art and science of food preservation. Its historical roots highlight the ingenuity of early civilizations in extending the shelf life of perishable foods, while its cultural significance underscores the diversity and richness of global culinary traditions. The process of pickling transforms simple ingredients into complex, flavorful foods that offer enhanced nutritional benefits and contribute to a sustainable food system. As we continue to rediscover and reinvent these ancient techniques, pickling remains a vibrant and relevant part of our culinary heritage, connecting us to our past and offering endless possibilities for innovation and exploration in the kitchen.

Types of pickling (vinegar-based, salt-based)

Pickling, a method steeped in history, serves to preserve food and enhance its flavors. This ancient technique, which has been practiced worldwide for thousands of years, involves submerging foods in a solution or mixture that prevents spoilage, thereby extending shelf life. The essence of pickling lies in its ability to inhibit the development of bacteria that cause food to decay, making it a crucial food preservation method before modern refrigeration's advent. Among the various pickling methods, vinegar-based and salt-based pickling stand out for their unique processes and the distinct flavors they impart to the preserved foods. This section delves into the nuances of these two primary types of pickling, exploring their methods, benefits, and the diverse culinary traditions they encompass.

Vinegar-based pickling, perhaps the most widely recognized form, utilizes vinegar as the primary preservative agent. This method involves immersing foods in a mixture of vinegar, water, and often, various seasonings and spices to enhance flavor. The acetic acid in vinegar is the key component that prevents microbial growth, effectively preserving the food. Vinegar-based pickles can range from the simple, like dill cucumbers, to the complex, incorporating a variety of spices and flavors. The process is relatively quick, with some pickles ready to eat in just a few days, though others may benefit from weeks or months of aging to develop their flavors fully. The acidic environment not only preserves the food but also imparts a tangy taste, transforming the texture and flavor profile of the original ingredients. This method is popular for pickling vegetables, fruits, and even some types of fish, offering a versatility that is celebrated in cuisines around the globe.

On the other hand, salt-based pickling relies on salt rather than vinegar to create an environment inhospitable to spoilage-causing bacteria. This method can be categorized into two main processes: brining, where food is submerged in a saltwater solution, and dry salting, where salt is applied directly to the food. Both of these processes draw moisture out of the food, creating a highly saline environment that inhibits the growth of harmful microbes. The osmosis process plays a crucial role in salt-based pickling, with the salt drawing water out of the microbial cells, effectively dehydrating and killing them. Over time, the food becomes preserved in the absence of these spoilage-causing bacteria. Salt-based pickling is often associated with the fermentation process, where naturally occurring or added bacteria convert sugars in the food into lactic acid, further preserving and flavoring the food. This method is traditional for fermenting vegetables, such as sauerkraut from cabbage and kimchi from a variety of vegetables, offering a depth of flavor and increased nutritional value, including probiotics.

The contrast between vinegar-based and salt-based pickling is in the methods and ingredients used and the resulting flavors and textures. Vinegar pickles tend to be crisp and tangy, with the acidity of the vinegar shining through as the dominant flavor profile. Depending on the added spices and seasonings, these pickles can be sweet or savory. Salt-based pickles, especially those that undergo fermentation, develop a complex, sour flavor over time, with a depth that vinegar-based pickles typically do not achieve. The textures can also vary, with salt-fermented pickles often softer than their vinegar-preserved counterparts.

Beyond their culinary applications, vinegar and salt-based pickling have significant cultural and historical significance. These methods have allowed communities to preserve seasonal bounty for consumption during scarce times, contributing to food security and sustainability. Additionally, pickling has been a means of transporting food over long distances, enabling exploration and trade. From the kimchi of Korea to the pickled herring of Scandinavia, pickled foods are deeply embedded in the culinary heritage of many cultures, each with its unique methods, flavors, and traditions.

In modern times, the interest in pickling has seen a resurgence, not only for its practical benefits in preserving food but also for the health benefits associated with fermented foods. The probiotics found in salt-fermented pickles are known to support gut health, highlighting the importance of these traditional methods in contemporary diets. Moreover, the art of pickling has become a creative outlet for chefs and home cooks alike, experimenting with flavors and techniques to produce gourmet pickles that elevate the dining experience.

In conclusion, vinegar-based and salt-based pickling are two fundamental methods that have played a vital role in food preservation and culinary traditions worldwide. Each technique offers its unique benefits, from the tangy crispness of vinegar pickles to the complex flavors of salt-fermented foods. As we continue to explore and appreciate the rich tapestry of pickling traditions, it becomes evident that these methods are more than just ways to preserve food; they are expressions of culture, history, and the ingenuity of human culinary practices.

Equipment needed for pickling

The art of pickling, a practice as ancient as civilization itself, requires not just skill and knowledge but also specific equipment to ensure success and safety. This process, which has been perfected over millennia, allows for preserving a wide array of foods, extending their shelf life and enhancing their flavors. Whether engaging in vinegar- or salt-based pickling, the enthusiast must gather a collection of tools and containers to transform fresh ingredients into tangy, savory, or sweet preserved delights. This section explores the essential equipment needed for pickling, underlining the importance of each item in the pickling process.

At the heart of the pickler's toolkit are the containers used for both fermenting and storing the pickled goods. Glass jars, traditionally known as Mason jars, are widely favored for their non-reactive nature, which ensures that the acidic content of the pickles does not corrode the container. These jars come in various sizes, accommodating everything from small batches of garlic cloves to large cucumbers or whole fruits. The transparency of glass also allows for easy monitoring of the pickling process, providing visual cues on the progress of fermentation or the state of preservation. These jars must be equipped with tight-fitting lids to seal the contents away from air, which can introduce unwanted bacteria or yeasts that might spoil the food.

Beyond jars, ceramic crocks are another option, particularly for large-scale or traditional salt-based fermentations, such as sauerkraut or kimchi. These heavy, sturdy containers offer excellent conditions for anaerobic fermentation, keeping the contents submerged and protected from air exposure. The use of weights, often made from the same ceramic material, is necessary to submerge the vegetables under the brine, preventing the growth of mold or bacteria on exposed parts.

The preparation of ingredients for pickling demands precision, for which various kitchen tools are needed. A sharp knife or a mandoline slicer allows for the ingredients to be cut uniformly, ensuring even pickling and an aesthetically pleasing result. Cutting the food into consistent shapes and sizes makes the jars more attractive and affects the pickling process itself, as smaller or thinner pieces will pickle faster than larger chunks. Additionally, measuring cups and spoons are indispensable for accurately preparing the pickling brine or vinegar solution, ensuring the correct balance of salt, sugar, vinegar, and water. This balance is crucial for creating an environment where beneficial fermentation can occur or preservation can be achieved without the risk of spoilage.

For vinegar-based pickling, a non-reactive pot, such as stainless steel or enameled cookware, is essential for heating the pickling solution. Aluminum, copper, and cast iron pots should be avoided as they can react with the acidity of the vinegar, potentially contaminating the pickles with metals and altering the taste. The heating process not only dissolves the salt and sugar but also helps to infuse the spices into the vinegar, creating a flavorful brine that will imbue the pickles with its character.

Canning equipment, including a water bath canner or a large, deep pot with a rack, is necessary for those who wish to store their pickles over an extended period. The process of water bath canning, applicable primarily to vinegar-based pickles, involves boiling the filled and sealed jars to ensure a vacuum seal and to kill off any remaining bacteria that could spoil the food. This method extends the shelf life of the pickles, allowing them to be stored at room temperature until opened.

Other useful tools for pickling include a wide-mouth funnel, which facilitates the clean transfer of brine and vegetables into jars, and tongs or jar lifters, which are essential for safely handling hot jars during the canning process. A bubble remover, or a simple non-metallic spatula, can be used to release air bubbles trapped in the jar before sealing, ensuring a tighter pack and reducing the risk of spoilage.

In conclusion, the equipment needed for pickling, from jars and crocks to knives, measuring tools, and canning gear, is fundamental to the success of the preservation process. Each item plays a specific role in ensuring the pickled products' safety, efficiency, and quality. With the right tools at hand, enthusiasts can embark on the rewarding journey of pickling, exploring the rich flavors and traditions of this ancient practice. As the pickler becomes more experienced, they may find that the initial investment in quality equipment enhances their craft and deepens their connection to the timeless art of preserving food.

What is fermenting?

Fermenting is a transformative process that cultures around the world have harnessed for thousands of years, not only as a means of preserving food but also for enhancing its nutritional value, flavor, and digestibility. This biological phenomenon, driven by microorganisms such as bacteria, yeasts, and molds, breaks down food components like sugars and starches into alcohol, gases, or organic acids. The result is a diverse array of fermented products, from the tangy depths of sauerkraut and the spicy complexity of kimchi to the refreshing effervescence of kombucha and the robust savoriness of soy sauce. This section explores the art and science of fermenting, delving into its principles, benefits, and its integral role in culinary traditions and human health.

At its core, fermenting is a natural preservation method that extends the shelf life of foods by developing an environment hostile to harmful bacteria. The process typically begins spontaneously, triggered by microorganisms naturally present on the surface of food or in the air. However, it can also be controlled and directed by adding specific cultures known as starters. These starters, which can be carefully selected strains of bacteria or yeasts, initiate the fermentation process, steering it towards desired outcomes regarding flavor, texture, and nutritional content. The anaerobic conditions created during fermentation are crucial, as they encourage the development of beneficial microbes while inhibiting the proliferation of spoilage-causing organisms and pathogens.

The chemical transformations that occur during fermentation do more than just preserve food. They also unlock nutritional benefits, making fermented foods a vital component of a healthy diet. For instance, fermentation can enhance nutrients' bioavailability, making them more accessible to the body. It also increases the levels of helpful bacteria in the gut when consumed, contributing to a balanced microbiome, improved digestion, and a strengthened immune system. Moreover, fermentation generates additional nutrients and bioactive compounds, such as B vitamins, omega-3 fatty acids, and antioxidants, further enriching the food's nutritional profile.

Beyond nutrition, the appeal of fermented foods lies in their unique flavors and textures, which result from the complex interactions between food components and fermenting microorganisms. These microbes produce a range of substances, including organic acids, alcohols, and esters, that contribute to the distinctive tastes and aromas of fermented products. This diversity enriches the culinary palette and allows for cultural expression through food, with each culture developing its fermentation traditions based on local ingredients, climatic conditions, and historical practices.

The fermenting process is as varied as the foods it produces, with different methods suited to different types of food. Lactic acid fermentation, one of the most common types, involves bacteria converting sugars into lactic acid, creating tangy flavors and preserving the food. This method is used in making yogurt, kefir, sauerkraut, and pickles. Alcoholic fermentation, driven by yeasts, transforms sugars into alcohol and carbon dioxide, as seen in beer, wine, and bread production. Acetic acid fermentation turns alcohol into vinegar, adding sourness to foods and offering preservative qualities. Each of these fermentation types showcases the versatility of the process and its ability to adapt to various culinary needs and preferences.

The significance of fermenting extends beyond the kitchen and the dining table. It represents a sustainable approach to food consumption and preservation, reducing waste by utilizing surplus produce and enhancing food security by allowing for the storage of perishable items. In a world grappling with the challenges of feeding a growing population and minimizing environmental impact, the practice of fermenting offers valuable lessons in resourcefulness and sustainability.

Furthermore, the resurgence of interest in traditional fermenting techniques in recent years highlights a collective desire to reconnect with the roots of our food systems. This renewed appreciation reflects a broader movement towards whole, unprocessed foods and a recognition of the intricate connections between diet, health, and the environment. As more people seek to incorporate fermented foods into their diets, there is an opportunity to explore the rich tapestry of global fermentation practices, learning from the wisdom of past generations while innovating for the future.

In conclusion, fermenting is a multifaceted process that transcends its primary function of food preservation. It is a bridge between art and science, tradition and innovation, offering a window into societies' cultural heritage while providing tangible health benefits and contributing to a sustainable food future. As we continue to explore the possibilities of fermentation, we unlock the potential for a deeper understanding of our relationship with food, health, and the environment, embracing the microbial alchemy that transforms the ordinary into the extraordinary.

How fermentation works

Fermentation is a fascinating biological process that has been exploited by humans for thousands of years, enabling food preservation, nutritional value enhancement, and unique flavors and textures. This process, which seems almost magical, is a complex biochemical reaction facilitated by microorganisms such as bacteria, yeasts, and molds. Understanding how fermentation works involves delving into the intricacies of microbial metabolism and the conditions that favor transforming simple ingredients into fermented foods and beverages. This section explores the science behind fermentation, outlining the stages of microbial growth, the types of fermentation, and the factors that influence the success of this ancient yet continually evolving practice.

At its core, fermentation is the metabolic process by which microorganisms convert carbohydrates, such as sugars and starches, into alcohol or acids anaerobically, meaning without the presence of oxygen. This conversion is not merely incidental; it is a survival strategy for the microorganisms, allowing them to extract energy from nutrients under conditions where oxygen, the electron acceptor in aerobic respiration, is scarce or absent. The byproducts of this metabolic activity, including lactic acid, acetic acid, and ethanol, depending on the type of microorganism and the conditions of fermentation, are what inhibit the growth of spoilage-causing and pathogenic organisms, thus preserving the food.

The process begins when a food item rich in carbohydrates is introduced to a fermentation agent, which could be naturally occurring microbes in the environment or those added as a starter culture. These microbes feast on the sugars in the food, initiating fermentation. In lactic acid fermentation, for example, lactobacilli bacteria convert sugars into lactic acid, imparting a tangy flavor to the food and lowering its pH, making the environment inhospitable for harmful bacteria. This type of fermentation is responsible for the creation of yogurt, sauerkraut, and sourdough bread.

Alcoholic fermentation, primarily carried out by yeasts, particularly Saccharomyces cerevisiae, follows a similar principle but yields ethanol as well as carbon dioxide as the main products. This process is central to producing beer, wine, and spirits. The carbon dioxide generated during fermentation is what causes bread to rise, as the gas becomes trapped in the dough's gluten network, creating a light and airy texture.

Another significant type of fermentation is acetic acid fermentation, where acetic acid bacteria (AAB) oxidize alcohol into acetic acid under aerobic conditions. This process is used to produce vinegar, a staple in culinary applications worldwide. The transformation from alcohol to vinegar showcases a different aspect of fermentation, emphasizing the versatility and range of conditions under which fermentation can occur.

The success of fermentation depends on several factors, including temperature, pH, salinity, and the absence or presence of oxygen. Each microorganism involved in fermentation has specific requirements for optimal growth and activity. For instance, lactobacilli thrive in warmer temperatures and slightly acidic conditions, making them well-suited for fermenting vegetables and dairy. Conversely, Yeasts prefer slightly cooler temperatures and neutral to slightly acidic pH levels, aligning with their role in bread making and alcoholic fermentation.

Control over these conditions is crucial for ensuring a successful fermentation process. Temperature, for example, affects the rate of microbial metabolism; too cold, and the microbes become dormant, too hot, and they may die or produce undesirable flavors. Similarly, the fermentation environment's pH can affect the final product's safety and quality, with highly acidic conditions favoring the preservation of food but potentially inhibiting the growth of desired microorganisms.

The stages of microbial growth during fermentation – lag, exponential, stationary, and death phases – also play a critical role in the process. Initially, microbes acclimatize to their new environment, experiencing little to no growth (lag phase). Once adapted, they begin to reproduce rapidly, consuming available nutrients and producing fermentation byproducts (exponential phase). As nutrients become scarce and waste products accumulate, growth rates slow, and the population stabilizes (stationary phase). Eventually, the depletion of nutrients and the buildup of toxic byproducts lead to a decline in the microbial population (death phase).

In conclusion, the process of fermentation is a delicate dance of microbial activity, governed by the interplay of environmental conditions and the innate metabolic pathways of the microorganisms involved. These tiny but powerful agents of change transform raw ingredients into products of increased preservation, enhanced nutrition, and complex flavors through their ability to convert carbohydrates into acids, alcohols, and gases. The science behind fermentation illuminates this ancient practice's workings and underscores its continued relevance and adaptability in contemporary food production and culinary innovation. As we deepen our understanding of how fermentation works, we unlock new possibilities for creating sustainable, healthful, and diverse food systems.

Equipment needed for fermenting

Fermentation, a process steeped in history and tradition, transforms simple ingredients into complex flavors through the magic of microbial activity. This ancient technique, celebrated across cultures for its ability to preserve food and enhance nutritional value, requires skill, knowledge, and specific equipment to ensure success and safety. As interest in homemade fermented foods continues to rise, understanding the essential tools and containers needed becomes paramount for both novices and seasoned fermenters alike. This section delves into the fundamental equipment necessary for fermenting a wide array of foods and beverages, highlighting the importance of each component in facilitating the fermentation process.

Central to the art of fermenting is the container in which the fermentation takes place. Glass jars, often referred to by the brand name Mason jars, are among the most famous choices due to their non-reactive nature, ensuring that no unwanted flavors are imparted to the food. These jars come in various sizes, accommodating everything from small batches of fermented hot sauce to larger quantities of sauerkraut or kimchi. The transparency of glass also allows for easy monitoring of the fermentation process, providing visual cues to the fermenter about the progress of the microbial activity. These jars must be equipped with airtight lids to create an anaerobic environment essential for successful fermentation, yet they must also allow for the release of carbon dioxide gas that accumulates during the process.

For larger scale or traditional fermentations, ceramic crocks offer an ideal solution. These vessels have been used for centuries in various cultures for fermenting vegetables, such as sauerkraut and pickles. Crocks are typically heavier and provide a more stable environment for long-term fermentations. Many come with weights that fit inside the crock to submerge the fermenting food beneath the brine, thereby preventing exposure to air, which can lead to mold growth. Using a water seal in some crocks also allows gases to escape while preventing outside air from entering, maintaining the necessary anaerobic conditions.

In addition to containers, a variety of tools aid in the preparation and maintenance of fermentations. A food-grade plastic or stainless steel funnel can be invaluable for transferring brine or liquid ferments into jars without spillage, ensuring a clean and efficient process. Similarly, a tamper or pounder, often made of wood or plastic, is essential for tightly packing vegetables into jars or crocks. This action helps to remove air pockets and ensures that the produce is submerged in brine, which is crucial for preventing spoilage and ensuring even fermentation.

The role of weights in fermenting cannot be overstated. Whether using specially designed glass weights, ceramic plates, or clean, boiled stones, the objective is to keep fermenting foods fully submerged under the liquid to prevent mold and unwanted bacteria from proliferating on the surface. For those using Mason jars, silicone or plastic fermentation lids that feature airlocks or one-way valves effectively release gas while keeping air out, streamlining the fermentation process and reducing the risk of contamination.

Temperature and humidity control devices, though not essential, can significantly enhance the fermenter's ability to maintain optimal conditions for fermentation. Thermometers and hygrometers help monitor the environment, especially when fermenting temperature-sensitive products like kombucha or certain cheeses. For advanced home fermenters, temperature-controlled fermentation chambers or converted refrigerators offer precise control over the fermentation environment, enabling consistent results and exploring more complex fermentation projects.

Lastly, clean, non-reactive utensils such as stainless steel spoons, ladles, and knives are crucial for preparing ingredients and handling fermented foods. Ensuring that all equipment is thoroughly sanitized before use is paramount to prevent the introduction of harmful bacteria that could spoil the fermentation. This emphasis on cleanliness extends to the fermenter's hands and workspace, highlighting the importance of good hygiene practices in successful fermenting.

In conclusion, the equipment needed for fermenting encompasses a range of containers, tools, and devices designed to create and maintain the ideal conditions for microbial activity. From glass jars and ceramic crocks to weights, airlocks, and temperature control systems, each element plays a critical role in the fermentation process, contributing to the final product's safety, efficiency, and quality. As interest in fermentation continues to grow, fueled by its health benefits and the desire for culinary exploration, the right equipment empowers enthusiasts to delve deeper into this ancient practice, unlocking the limitless potential of fermented foods and beverages. Whether a beginner or an experienced fermenter, investing in the appropriate equipment is a step toward mastering the art and science of fermentation, enabling the creation of diverse, healthful, and flavorful fermented goods.

Key ingredients for pickling and fermenting

The art of pickling and fermenting is a testament to human ingenuity in preserving food, enhancing flavors, and enriching our diets with probiotics and nutrients. While varying greatly across cultures and recipes, these time-honored practices share a foundation in several key ingredients that catalyze the transformation of fresh produce into tangy, savory, or sweet preserves. This section delves into the essential components of pickling and fermenting, exploring their roles in these processes and how they contribute to the unique characteristics of the finished products.

At the heart of most pickling processes is vinegar, a versatile ingredient whose acidic nature is crucial for preserving food and inhibiting the growth of harmful bacteria. Vinegar, which is derived from the fermentation of ethanol by acetic acid bacteria, comes in various types, including apple cider, white, and rice vinegar, each imparting distinct flavors to the pickles. The high acidity of vinegar-based pickles ensures safety and longevity and contributes a sharp, tangy taste that defines many pickled products.

Equally fundamental to fermenting, particularly in the production of vegetables like sauerkraut and kimchi, is salt. Salt serves multiple functions: it draws moisture out of the food through osmosis, creating an environment where beneficial lactobacillus bacteria can thrive and ferment the food while inhibiting the growth of spoilage-causing microorganisms. The concentration of salt, alongside the specific conditions under which fermentation occurs, determines the fermented product's texture, flavor, and safety. In pickling and fermenting, salt is not merely a seasoning but a critical component of the preservation process.

Water, often overlooked, is another key ingredient, especially in brine-based pickles and ferments. The water quality can significantly affect the outcome of the fermentation process. Chlorinated tap water, for instance, can inhibit the growth of beneficial bacteria and yeasts, making it essential to use filtered or spring water to ensure the best results. In pickling, water is mixed with vinegar and salt to create a brine in which the produce is submerged, while in fermenting, it is used to dissolve salt and cover the produce, keeping it anaerobic and safe from spoilage.

Sugar, while not essential in all recipes, plays a significant role in many pickling and fermenting processes. In pickling, sugar balances the acidity of vinegar, adding a complexity to the flavor profile of the final product. In fermenting, sugar can provide an additional source of carbohydrates for fermentation microbes, accelerating the fermentation process and contributing to the development of flavors. The type of sugar used, from white granulated to brown sugar or honey, can influence the taste and character of the finished product.

Spices and herbs are the soul of pickling and fermenting, introducing an array of flavors that transform the preserved food into culinary delights. Typical spices used in pickling include mustard seeds, peppercorns, dill, and coriander, each adding distinct notes to the pickles. Herbs like dill, bay leaves, and tarragon, as well as garlic and chili peppers, are frequently used to infuse the pickles with their aromatic qualities. In fermenting, particularly in dishes like kimchi, a combination of spices, including chili powder, ginger, and garlic, not only flavors the ferment but can also have antimicrobial properties that support the fermentation process.

Starter cultures are sometimes used in fermenting to kickstart the process, especially in products like yogurt, kefir, and certain types of cheese. These cultures contain specific strains of bacteria or yeasts that are known to produce desirable flavors and textures. While many vegetable ferments rely on the natural bacteria present on the produce's surface, using starter cultures can offer more control over the fermentation process, leading to consistent and predictable results.

In conclusion, the key ingredients for pickling and fermenting—vinegar, salt, water, sugar, spices and herbs, and sometimes starter cultures—form the foundation upon which the vast and varied world of preserved foods is built. Each ingredient plays a specific and crucial role in the preservation process, contributing to the final product's safety, flavor, texture, and nutritional value. Understanding these ingredients and their functions allows for the successful preservation of food and the creative expression of flavors and traditions. As the interest in homemade pickles and ferments continues to grow, these fundamental components serve as the building blocks for experimentation and innovation, enabling home cooks and artisans alike to explore the endless possibilities of pickling and fermenting.

CHAPTER III

Pickling Recipes

Classic pickled cucumbers

Classic pickled cucumbers, a staple in pantries around the globe, epitomize the timeless art of pickling, a method of preservation steeped in history and tradition. This simple yet profound culinary practice transforms the humble cucumber into a tangy, flavorful delicacy, enhancing its longevity and nutritional value. Creating classic pickled cucumbers is a dance of balance and flavor, involving a symphony of ingredients, techniques, and patience. This section delves into the history, process, and cultural significance of classic pickled cucumbers, offering insights into their enduring popularity and versatility in cuisines worldwide.

The art of pickling cucumbers dates back thousands of years, with evidence suggesting its practice in ancient Mesopotamia. The technique likely arose out of necessity, as early agricultural societies sought methods to preserve their crops beyond the growing season. Over time, pickling became a refined craft, spreading across empires and trade routes, each culture adding its signature to the primary process. In Eastern Europe, for example, dill and garlic became synonymous with pickled cucumbers, while in Asia, spicy and sweet variations emerged. Despite these regional variations, the essence of pickling cucumbers remains a shared global heritage, bridging cultures through the universal desire to savor the bounty of the harvest year-round.

Making classic pickled cucumbers begins with selecting the correct type of cucumber. Small, firm cucumbers, often labeled as "pickling cucumbers," are ideal due to their thin skins and tiny seeds, allowing them to absorb the brine more effectively. The cucumbers are then cleaned and often sliced or left whole, depending on preference and tradition. Preparing the brine is the next critical step, a mixture of water, vinegar, and salt that serves as the pickling liquid. The vinegar's acidity and the brine's salinity are critical to inhibiting bacterial growth, ensuring the cucumbers are preserved safely.

Seasonings and spices play a pivotal role in defining the flavor profile of classic pickled cucumbers. Dill, garlic, mustard seeds, peppercorns, and bay leaves are among the most common additions, each imparting distinct notes that complement the cucumber's natural crispness. The choice and combination of spices can vary widely, reflecting personal tastes and regional preferences. This versatility is part of what makes pickled cucumbers so beloved; they can be customized to suit any palate, from intensely sour to sweetly spiced.

Once the cucumbers are prepared and the brine is seasoned, they are packed into sterilized jars, and the hot brine is poured over them, ensuring they are completely submerged. The jars are then sealed and left to cool before being stored in a cool, dark place to ferment. Over the following days or weeks, the cucumbers undergo a transformation, as the acidic environment of the brine works to pickle them. The length of this process can vary, with some preferring a crunchier, fresher taste, while others may opt for a more extended fermentation period, allowing deeper flavors to develop.

The cultural significance of classic pickled cucumbers extends beyond their taste and preservation benefits. They have become symbolic of hospitality and tradition in many cultures, complementing meals, a staple in festive celebrations, and a cherished homemade gift. In Eastern Europe, no feast is complete without a plate of pickled cucumbers, while in the United States, they are a beloved side dish at summer barbecues and a classic ingredient in sandwiches. Their universal appeal lies in their taste and ability to evoke memories of family, tradition, and the simple joy of sharing a meal.

Moreover, classic pickled cucumbers offer nutritional benefits, including vitamins and minerals preserved during pickling. Fermentation also encourages the growth of beneficial bacteria, or probiotics, contributing to gut health when consumed in moderation. This combination of flavor, tradition, and health benefits has cemented the classic pickled cucumber's place in the pantheon of preserved foods, a testament to the enduring legacy of pickling.

In conclusion, classic pickled cucumbers embody the essence of pickling, a culinary tradition that transcends time and geography. By preserving cucumbers in a brine of vinegar, salt, and spices, generations of cooks have created a food that delights the palate, nourishes the body, and connects us to our cultural heritage. While straightforward, the process of making classic pickled cucumbers demands care, knowledge, and a respect for the craft that has been passed down through the ages. As we continue to explore and celebrate the diversity of pickled foods, the classic pickled cucumber stands as a reminder of the power of preservation to transform the ordinary into the extraordinary, uniting us across cultures and generations through the universal language of food.

Pickled carrots with ginger

Pickled carrots with ginger represent a delightful fusion of flavors and traditions, blending the earthy sweetness of carrots with the spicy warmth of ginger, all enveloped in a tangy pickling brine. This delicacy, though simple in its composition, carries with it a rich tapestry of culinary innovation and cross-cultural exchange. As an exploration of the art of pickling, this section delves into the origins, preparation, and cultural significance of pickled carrots with ginger, shedding light on how this humble preserve has become a beloved condiment and ingredient in kitchens around the globe.

The practice of pickling, a method of preservation that dates back thousands of years, has seen countless variations depending on the ingredients available, regional taste preferences, and culinary traditions. Carrots, with their natural sweetness and crisp texture, have long been a popular choice for pickling. When combined with ginger, a root known for its medicinal properties and bold flavor, the result is a pickled concoction that is both refreshing and comforting. This combination likely owes its existence to the confluence of different culinary traditions, where the use of spices such as ginger to enhance and preserve food led to the creation of recipes that celebrate the ingredients' complementary flavors.

Making pickled carrots with ginger begins with selecting young, tender carrots. Depending on preference, these are peeled and sliced into sticks or rounds to ensure even absorption of the pickling liquid. Fresh and aromatic ginger is typically julienned or finely sliced to distribute its pungent flavor throughout the jar. The brine, a critical component of any pickle, is a mixture of vinegar, water, sugar, and salt. The vinegar, usually white or apple cider, provides the acidity necessary for preservation, while sugar balances the tang with a hint of sweetness. Salt, in addition to its preservative qualities, enhances the overall taste of the pickle.

Spices and seasonings are pivotal in defining the character of pickled carrots with ginger. Mustard seeds, peppercorns, and coriander seeds are common additions, offering depth and complexity to the brine. Garlic cloves and chili flakes may also be included for an extra layer of flavor, creating a balance between the heat of the ginger and the sweetness of the carrots. The choice of spices can vary widely, reflecting personal tastes and the influence of regional pickling traditions.

Once prepared, the carrots and ginger are tightly packed into sterilized jars, and the hot brine is poured over them, ensuring all pieces are submerged. The jars are then sealed and left to cool before being stored in a cool, dark place to ferment. The fermentation process permits the flavors to meld and deepen, transforming the raw ingredients into a harmonious blend of sweet, spicy, and tangy. The pickles can be enjoyed after a few days, though allowing them to sit longer will result in a more pronounced flavor profile.

Pickled carrots with ginger are more than just a condiment; they are a testament to the versatility and creativity inherent in pickling. They can be served as a side dish, adding a refreshing crunch and zesty flavor to meals, or used as an ingredient in salads, sandwiches, and wraps. Their vibrant color and appealing aesthetics also make them a visually striking addition to any dining table, enhancing the sensory experience of eating.

Beyond their culinary appeal, pickled carrots with ginger embody the fusion of health and taste. Carrots are a high source of beta-carotene, fiber, vitamins, and minerals, while ginger is renowned for its anti-inflammatory and digestive properties. While altering the texture and flavor of these ingredients, the pickling process preserves their nutritional benefits, offering a delicious way to incorporate healthy elements into the diet.

The cultural significance of pickled carrots with ginger extends beyond their health benefits, reflecting a broader appreciation for preserved foods across different cultures. This pickle symbolizes the ingenuity of traditional preservation methods, adapted and reinvented by each generation to suit changing tastes and dietary needs. It represents a connection to the past, a celebration of seasonal bounty, and a recognition of the simple joy of creating as well as sharing food.

In conclusion, pickled carrots with ginger are a vibrant expression of the global tapestry of pickling traditions, uniting the sweetness of carrots with the piquant kick of ginger in a tangy brine. This pickle encapsulates the essence of culinary creativity, the importance of preservation, and the joy of eating foods that are as nourishing as they are flavorful. As we explore the endless possibilities of pickling, recipes like pickled carrots with ginger remind us of the power of simple ingredients to evoke complex tastes and memories, bridging cultures and generations through the shared experience of good food.

Spicy pickled green beans

Spicy pickled green beans, a fiery twist on traditional pickling, embody the harmonious blend of heat, tang, and crisp freshness that has captivated palates across cultures. This condiment, known for its vibrant flavor and satisfying crunch, offers a testament to the versatility of pickling as both an art and a science. Spicy pickled green beans transform a simple vegetable into an extraordinary culinary delight by infusing the humble green bean with a bold combination of spices and vinegar. This section explores the origins, preparation, and cultural significance of spicy pickled green beans, shedding light on their enduring popularity and their unique place in the world of preserved foods.

Pickling vegetables dates back thousands of years, with each culture adapting the method to suit local tastes and available ingredients. Green beans, with their firm texture and mild flavor, provide an ideal canvas for pickling, absorbing the brine flavors while retaining their crispness. Adding spice to the pickling liquid is a relatively modern innovation, reflecting a growing desire for more complex and bold flavors in preserved foods. Spicy pickled green beans, often referred to as "dilly beans" in some regions, mainly when dill is a featured ingredient, marry the traditional technique of vinegar preservation with the heat of chili peppers and the aromatic depth of spices such as garlic, mustard seeds, and black peppercorns.

The process of making spicy pickled green beans begins with the selection of fresh, young beans. These are cleaned and trimmed, then packed into sterilized jars along with the chosen spices. Depending on the desired heat level, common additions include fresh dill, garlic cloves, and slices of hot peppers, such as jalapeños or habaneros. The brine, a critical component of any pickle, is a mixture of vinegar and water, to which salt and sometimes sugar are added. The vinegar not only imparts the characteristic tangy flavor but also creates an acidic setting that inhibits the growth of spoilage-causing bacteria, ensuring the safety and longevity of the pickles.

Once the beans and spices are in place, the hot brine is poured over them, filling the jars to just below the rim. This step is followed by sealing the jars tightly and processing them in a boiling water bath, further ensuring the destruction of any potentially harmful microorganisms. The jars are then left to cool and stored in a cool, dark place, allowing the flavors to meld and develop over time. The result is a crunchy, spicy pickle that can be enjoyed being a side dish, a snack, or an addition to salads and sandwiches.

Spicy pickled green beans are more than just a tasty condiment; they represent a confluence of tradition and innovation. The technique of pickling, which has its roots in the necessity of preserving food for leaner times, is given new life by including bold spices and flavors. This adaptation speaks to the evolving nature of culinary practices, where food preservation intersects with the desire for diverse and vibrant taste experiences. Moreover, the choice of green beans as the base for these pickles reflects a broader trend toward exploring the pickling potential of a wide range of vegetables, beyond the cucumbers and cabbages traditionally associated with this method.

The cultural significance of spicy pickled green beans extends beyond their role as a food item. They embody the spirit of home canning and preserving, a practice that has seen a resurgence in popularity as individuals seek to reconnect with the origins of their food and embrace more sustainable eating habits. Making spicy pickled green beans at home offers a tangible link to the past, a time when preserving the harvest was a communal activity that brought families and communities together. It also represents an act of creativity and personal expression, as each batch can be customized with different levels of spice, types of vinegar, and combinations of herbs and seasonings.

In conclusion, spicy pickled green beans are a vibrant testament to the enduring appeal of pickled foods. They bridge the gap between traditional preservation techniques and contemporary flavor preferences, offering a spicy, tangy, and crunchy snack that appeals to modern tastes while honoring the age-old practice of pickling. As a culinary creation, they exemplify the potential for innovation within the framework of tradition, showcasing how simple ingredients can be changed into something extraordinary. Through the lens of spicy pickled green beans, we gain knowledge into the historical, cultural, and gastronomic significance of pickling, a process that continues to enrich our culinary landscape with flavors that are as diverse and dynamic as the people who enjoy them.

Pickled beets with herbs

Pickled beets with herbs are a culinary delight that marry the earthy sweetness of beets with the aromatic freshness of herbs, all encapsulated within the tangy embrace of a vinegar brine. This vibrant preserve not only adds a splash of color to any plate but also brings with it layers of flavor and nutritional benefits. The tradition of pickling beets is steeped in history, tracing back to times when preserving the bounty of harvest was not just for culinary enjoyment but a necessity for survival. This section explores the rich tapestry of pickled beets with herbs, delving into their preparation, cultural significance, and the subtle artistry of balancing flavors in this beloved preserve.

The process of creating pickled beets with herbs begins with a careful selection of ingredients. Fresh, firm beets are essential, as their texture and flavor are the foundation upon which the pickle is built. The beets are washed, and often roasted, a step that enhances their natural sweetness by concentrating their sugars. Once cooled, the skins are removed, and the beets are sliced or cut into wedges, ready to be immersed in the pickling liquid.

The brine, a mixture of vinegar, water, sugar, and salt, acts as the preserving medium. Vinegar's high acidity inhibits the growth of spoilage-causing microorganisms, while sugar and salt balance the acidity, enhancing the beets' natural flavors. The choice of vinegar can vary from the sharpness of white vinegar to the mellow tones of apple cider vinegar, each lending its unique character to the final product.

Herbs play a pivotal role in distinguishing pickled beets, adding layers of flavor that complement the sweetness of the beets. With its feathery fronds and sweet, aromatic profile, Dill is a classic pairing, while thyme offers subtle earthiness. With its piney fragrance, Rosemary can lend a robust undertone, and tarragon introduces a hint of anise. The choice of herbs can be tailored to personal taste or inspired by regional traditions, making each batch of pickled beets a reflection of individual or cultural culinary preferences.

The art of pickling beets with herbs lies in the ingredients and the method. The prepared beets are packed into sterilized jars along with the chosen herbs. The hot brine is then poured over the beets, ensuring they are fully submerged. The jars are sealed and left to cool before being stored to allow the flavors to meld. Over time, the beets absorb the tangy essence of the brine and the aromatic qualities of the herbs, transforming into a pickle that is at once sweet, tangy, and herbaceous.

Pickled beets with herbs are more than a testament to the art of preservation; they celebrate seasonal eating and sustainability. Beets, a root vegetable that stores well, become a canvas for the flavors of fresh herbs, allowing the tastes of summer and autumn to be savored throughout the year. Preserving seasonal produce is a tradition that spans cultures and generations, a testament to humanity's ingenuity in making the most of nature's bounty.

Culturally, pickled beets with herbs occupy a cherished place in the culinary heritage of many countries. They are a staple in Eastern Europe, often served alongside hearty meals, adding a refreshing contrast to rich dishes. In Scandinavian cuisine, they accompany fish, providing a bright counterpoint to the oily richness. Beyond their role as a side dish, pickled beets with herbs can be a vibrant addition to salads and sandwiches and even as a component in creative appetizers and cocktails, showcasing their versatility.

Another aspect of pickled beets' appeal is their nutritional profile. Beets are high in vitamins, minerals, as well as antioxidants, offering health benefits, including improved blood flow and lower blood pressure. While pickling alters their nutritional composition slightly, vinegar and herbs add digestive benefits, making pickled beets with herbs a healthful addition to the diet.

In conclusion, pickled beets with herbs are a harmonious blend of the earthy and the aromatic, a preserve that encapsulates the essence of the ingredients from which it is made. The process of making them is a ritual that celebrates the seasons, sustains culinary traditions, and delights the palate with its complex flavors. In each jar of pickled beets with herbs lies a story of cultural heritage, a tribute to the art of preservation, and a testament to the enduring appeal of simple ingredients transformed through the alchemy of pickling. As we explore and embrace traditional food preservation methods, pickled beets with herbs are a vibrant reminder of the beauty and bounty of nature, preserved in brine and enhanced with the fragrant touch of herbs.

Pickled onions with thyme

Pickled onions with thyme embody a culinary tradition that marries the sharp bite of onions with thyme's subtle, earthy notes, all nestled within the tangy embrace of vinegar. This preparation, a staple in many cultures, transcends mere preservation, becoming a delicacy that enhances myriad dishes with its vibrant flavors and textures. The process of pickling, an ancient method of food preservation, transforms the raw, pungent qualities of onions into something mellow, complex, and utterly delightful. This section explores the art and craft of creating pickled onions with thyme, delving into their preparation, cultural significance, and the myriad ways in which they enrich our culinary experiences.

The journey of crafting pickled onions with thyme begins with the selection of ingredients. Small, firm onions are preferred for their size, which allows them to absorb the pickling brine more effectively, and for their sweeter taste compared to larger varieties. Peeling and preparing these onions can be a labor of love, as their pungent aroma is released, laying the groundwork for their transformation. Thyme, an herb celebrated for its aromatic qualities and versatility, is chosen for its ability to infuse the onions with a subtle layer of flavor that complements their natural sweetness and the acidity of the vinegar.

The brine, a critical component in the pickling process, is a vinegar, water, salt, and sugar concoction. The vinegar, typically white or apple cider, acts as the preservative, creating an acidic environment in which bacteria cannot thrive. Salt and sugar are added for their preservative qualities and to balance the flavors, ensuring the final product is not overly acidic. Adding thyme to the brine introduces a herbal note that sets pickled onions apart, providing a depth of flavor that elevates them from a simple condiment to a gourmet ingredient.

Preparing pickled onions with thyme is a testament to the simplicity and elegance of pickling. The peeled onions are often blanched briefly in boiling water, a step that softens them and makes them more receptive to the brine. They are then packed into sterilized jars, along with sprigs of thyme, and the hot brine is poured over them, ensuring they are completely submerged. The jars are sealed and left to cool, then stored to allow the flavors to meld. Over time, the onions soften further, and the sharpness mellows, resulting in a tangy and sweet condiment, with the thyme providing a nuanced backdrop that enhances the overall flavor profile.

The cultural significance of pickled onions with thyme is rooted in the long history of pickling as a preservation method. Before the advent of modern refrigeration, pickling was one of the few ways to extend the shelf life of perishable ingredients. Over the centuries, this necessity evolved into a culinary art form, with each culture developing its own unique pickling traditions. Pickled onions, in particular, have found their place in various cuisines, celebrated for their versatility and ability to add brightness and complexity to dishes.

From a culinary perspective, pickled onions with thyme are remarkably versatile. They can be part of a charcuterie board, adding a tangy contrast to rich cheeses and cured meats. They make an excellent accompaniment to hearty stews and casseroles, where their acidity cuts through the richness of the dishes. In sandwiches and burgers, they provide a crisp, flavorful counterpoint to the other components. Moreover, they can be finely chopped and added to salads, salsas, and dressings, offering bursts of flavor that elevate the overall dish.

Beyond their culinary uses, pickled onions with thyme offer nutritional benefits. Onions are high in vitamins, minerals, as well as antioxidants, and their consumption has been associated to various health benefits, including enhanced heart health and reduced inflammation. Thyme adds its own set of medicinal properties, including antibacterial and antifungal effects. While altering some of the nutritional aspects of the onions, the pickling process preserves these benefits, making pickled onions with thyme a delicious addition to meals and a healthful one.

In conclusion, pickled onions with thyme are a celebration of the art of pickling, a technique that turns simple ingredients into something extraordinary. The process, rooted in necessity, has evolved into a culinary tradition that spans cultures and cuisines, offering a testament to the creativity and ingenuity of cooks throughout history. The combination of onions and thyme, preserved in vinegar, creates a versatile and flavorful condiment, capable of enhancing a wide array of dishes. As we explore and embrace traditional food preservation methods, pickled onions with thyme are a vibrant reminder of the beauty and bounty of nature, captured in a jar, ready to be enjoyed in countless meals.

Pickled cauliflower with turmeric

Pickled cauliflower with turmeric is a vibrant and healthful condiment that embodies the essence of traditional pickling techniques while embracing its key ingredients' bold flavors and nutritional benefits. This delightful preparation brings together the crisp, mild flavor of cauliflower with the earthy, pungent notes of turmeric, all preserved in a tangy vinegar brine. The result is a visually striking addition to any meal and a versatile and nutrient-rich side that complements a wide range of dishes. This section explores the origins, preparation, and cultural significance of pickled cauliflower with turmeric, shedding light on its enduring popularity and its unique place in the world of preserved foods.

The practice of pickling vegetables dates back thousands of years, serving as a crucial method for preserving the bounty of the harvest. With its dense, absorbent florets, Cauliflower is particularly well-suited to pickling, as it readily takes on the flavors of the brine and spices. Turmeric, a spice revered not only for its distinctive flavor and color but also for its anti-inflammatory and antioxidant properties, enhances the pickling liquid, imbuing the cauliflower with its bright golden hue and myriad health benefits. The combination of cauliflower and turmeric in a pickled preparation is a testament to the ingenuity of cooks seeking to elevate simple vegetables to something extraordinary.

Preparing pickled cauliflower with turmeric involves a few simple but precise steps. Fresh cauliflower is cut into florets, ensuring they are of a uniform size for even pickling. The brine, typically a mixture of vinegar, water, sugar, and salt, acts as the preserving medium, with vinegar's acidity creating an environment inhospitable to spoilage-causing bacteria. Turmeric is added to the brine, along with other spices such as mustard seeds, coriander seeds, and peppercorns, which contribute depth and complexity to the flavor profile. The inclusion of turmeric not only imparts a warm, earthy taste but also gives the cauliflower a striking golden color, making the finished product as visually appealing as it is delicious.

The cultural significance of pickled cauliflower with turmeric extends beyond its culinary uses, reflecting a broader appreciation for fermented and pickled foods across various traditions. In many cultures, pickled vegetables are a staple at meals, valued for their ability to enhance the flavors of dishes and provide a tangy contrast to richer foods. The addition of turmeric, a spice that has been employed for centuries in conventional medicine and cooking, particularly in South Asian as well as Middle Eastern cuisines, speaks to the global influences that shape contemporary food practices. This fusion of ingredients and techniques results in a pickle that is rooted in tradition and resonates with modern palates seeking healthful, flavorful options.

From a nutritional standpoint, pickled cauliflower with turmeric offers numerous benefits. Cauliflower is a cruciferous vegetable high in vitamins C and K, fiber, and antioxidants, which support overall health and may help minimize the risk of chronic diseases. Turmeric's active compound, curcumin, is recognized for its anti-inflammatory and antioxidant properties, potentially offering additional health benefits when consumed regularly. While the pickling process may alter some of the cauliflower's nutritional content, preserving these key ingredients in a vinegar brine ensures that their health benefits are retained, making pickled cauliflower with turmeric a nutritious addition to any diet.

Culinarily, pickled cauliflower with turmeric is incredibly versatile. It can be served as a condiment along with curries, rice dishes, and grilled meats, providing a refreshing, tangy counterpoint to rich flavors. It is also a colorful and flavorful addition to salads, sandwiches, and charcuterie boards, where its bright color and unique taste can elevate simple dishes to something special. This pickle's tangy, spicy flavor profile makes it a favorite among those who appreciate bold, vibrant foods that pack a nutritional punch.

In conclusion, pickled cauliflower with turmeric represents a harmonious blend of traditional pickling methods, global flavors, and nutritional wisdom. This preparation not only preserves the cauliflower in a way that enhances its natural flavors and textures but also leverages the health benefits of turmeric to create a condiment that is as healthful as it is delicious. The simplicity of its ingredients belies the complexity of its flavors and the depth of its cultural roots, making it a testament to the enduring appeal of pickled vegetables in cuisines worldwide. As we explore the rich tapestry of pickled and fermented foods, pickled cauliflower with turmeric stands out as a vibrant, healthful, and versatile addition to the culinary landscape, bridging the gap between tradition and modernity in every jar.

Pickled peppers in brine

Pickled peppers in brine epitomize the art of preservation that has been refined across cultures and generations, transforming the fiery heat and vibrant flavors of peppers into a tangy, shelf-stable delicacy. This practice not only extends the shelf life of these seasonal vegetables but also enhances their taste, making them a versatile ingredient in culinary traditions worldwide. The process of pickling peppers in a saltwater brine is an ancient technique, rooted in the necessity to preserve food for times of scarcity, which has evolved into a celebrated method for enriching the flavors of countless dishes. This section delves into the craft of creating pickled peppers in brine, exploring the intricacies of the process, the cultural significance of the product, and its enduring popularity in global cuisines.

The journey of pickling peppers begins with selecting fresh, firm peppers. From the mild bell pepper to the spicy habanero, the choice of pepper varies depending on the desired level of heat and the culinary traditions being honored. Once selected, the peppers are often sliced or pierced, a step that ensures the brine fully penetrates the vegetable, imbuing it with flavor and preserving its crisp texture. The brine, a simple yet precise concoction of water and salt, acts as the preserving medium. Its salinity inhibits the growth of spoilage-causing microorganisms, while allowing the beneficial lacto-fermentation process to occur, enhancing the peppers' natural flavors and adding a tangy depth.

In addition to salt, various flavorings and spices may be added to the brine to customize the pickled peppers. Garlic, dill, coriander, and mustard seeds are common additions, each contributing their unique profiles to the final product. The inclusion of these aromatics infuses the peppers with complex flavors, elevating them from merely preserved vegetables to a gourmet ingredient. The peppers and spices are packed into sterilized jars, and the brine is poured over them, ensuring they are fully submerged. The jars are then sealed and left to ferment at room temperature for a time ranging from a few days to several weeks, depending on the desired level of sourness and the specific recipe being followed.

The cultural significance of pickled peppers in brine is vast, reflecting the global diversity of pickling traditions. In Eastern European cuisines, pickled peppers are a staple, often served alongside meats and cheeses or incorporated into salads and stews. In the Americas, where peppers are indigenous, pickling has been a method of preservation for centuries, with each region developing its own variations that reflect local tastes and pepper varieties. The versatility of pickled peppers makes them a beloved ingredient in kitchens worldwide, used to add heat, tang, and flavor to dishes ranging from sandwiches and pizzas to tacos and curries.

Nutritionally, pickled peppers in brine offer several benefits. Peppers are high in vitamins A and C, antioxidants, and other nutrients that contribute to general health. The fermentation process also promotes the development of probiotics, beneficial bacteria that support gut health. While the salt content in brine-pickled peppers can be high, consuming them in moderation as part of a balanced diet allows one to enjoy their flavors and health benefits without concern.

From a culinary perspective, pickled peppers in brine are incredibly versatile. They can be used as a condiment, adding a tangy, spicy kick to burgers, hot dogs, and sandwiches, or as an ingredient in various dishes, where they lend their distinct flavor to salsas, relishes, and sauces. The brine itself, infused with the essence of the peppers and spices, can also be used in dressings, marinades, and cocktails, adding depth and complexity to a wide range of recipes.

In conclusion, pickled peppers in brine are a testament to the enduring art of preservation, a practice that not only extends the life of perishable foods but also enhances their flavors and nutritional value. This method, rooted in ancient traditions, continues to thrive in modern kitchens, bridging the gap between past and present, and between cultures across the globe. The simple yet profound process of fermenting peppers in a saltwater brine yields a product that is as versatile as it is delicious, beloved for its ability to spice up any meal with its tangy heat. As we continue to explore and celebrate the world's culinary diversity, pickled peppers in brine stand out as a vibrant, flavorful testament to the creativity and ingenuity of cooks everywhere, making them a cherished ingredient in the global pantry.

Pickled garlic cloves

Pickled garlic cloves represent a fascinating intersection of culinary tradition and innovation, where garlic's robust, pungent flavors meet the tangy sharpness of pickling brine, resulting in a versatile and healthful delicacy. This preservation method, which has roots in various cultures across the globe, transforms the often overpowering taste of raw garlic into something milder, sweeter, and more complex. The art of pickling garlic is a testament to humanity's ingenuity in food preservation, extending the shelf life of this staple ingredient and enhancing its culinary applications and nutritional benefits. This section delves into the intricacies of pickled garlic cloves, exploring the methods of preparation, cultural significance, and the myriad ways in which they enrich our culinary landscape.

The process of picking garlic begins with selecting high-quality, fresh garlic cloves. The cloves are peeled, a task that requires patience and care to ensure they remain intact. The choice of brine is crucial in determining the flavor profile of the pickled garlic; it typically consists of vinegar, water, and salt, with variations including sugar to balance the acidity. The acidity of the vinegar not only serves as a preservative but also softens the sharp bite of the garlic, making it more palatable and digestible.

Spices and herbs are often added to the brine to infuse the garlic with additional flavors. Classic additions include dill, mustard seeds, peppercorns, and bay leaves, each contributing their unique notes to the final product. More adventurous variations might incorporate chili flakes, rosemary, or thyme, allowing for a wide range of flavors that can be tailored to personal taste or specific culinary traditions. The garlic cloves and the chosen spices are packed into sterilized jars, and the hot brine is poured over them, ensuring they are completely submerged. The jars are then sealed and left to ferment, a process that can take from a few weeks to several months, depending on the desired level of pickling.

The cultural significance of pickled garlic is as diverse as the cuisines that embrace it. In many Mediterranean and Asian countries, garlic is a foundational ingredient and valued for its medicinal properties. The practice of pickling garlic in these regions is steeped in history, often associated with health benefits such as improved digestion and immunity. Pickled garlic is a common accompaniment to meals, serving as a flavor enhancer and digestive aid. Its use spans simple appetizers and side dishes to complex marinades and sauces, highlighting its versatility and importance in worldwide culinary traditions.

Nutritionally, pickled garlic retains many of the health benefits associated with raw garlic, including its anti-inflammatory, antibacterial, and antioxidant properties. Fermentation may also contribute additional health benefits, such as probiotics, which support gut health. However, it's important to note that the nutritional content can vary depending on the pickling method and ingredients used. Nonetheless, pickled garlic remains a healthful addition to the diet, offering a flavorful way to incorporate garlic's well-documented health benefits.

Culinarily, pickled garlic cloves are incredibly versatile, adding depth and subtlety to dishes that might be overwhelmed by raw garlic. Their milder flavor makes them suitable for a wide range of culinary applications, from being chopped and added to salads and dressings to serving as a tangy accompaniment to cheese and charcuterie boards. Pickled garlic can also be used as a flavorful garnish for cooked dishes, where it adds a burst of tangy garlic flavor without the raw bite. Furthermore, the brine from pickled garlic can be used in dressings, marinades, and sauces, adding complexity and tang to various recipes.

In conclusion, pickled garlic cloves are a remarkable example of how traditional food preservation techniques can enhance and transform the flavors of simple ingredients. The process of pickling garlic not only extends its shelf life but also opens up new culinary possibilities, allowing the distinctive taste of garlic to be enjoyed in a more subdued and nuanced form. The cultural and nutritional significance of pickled garlic underscores its value in cuisines worldwide, where it continues to be celebrated for its versatility, health benefits, as well as the depth of flavor it brings to dishes. As we continue to explore and appreciate the rich tapestry of global culinary traditions, pickled garlic cloves stand out as a testament to the enduring appeal of preserved foods and their ability to connect us to the past while inspiring future culinary innovations.

Mixed vegetable pickles

Mixed vegetable pickles, a vibrant tapestry of colors, textures, and flavors, encapsulate the essence of culinary diversity and preservation. This delightful medley, comprising a variety of vegetables steeped in a tangy brine, is more than just a condiment or side dish; it is a celebration of the harvest, a testament to the ingenuity of preservation methods, and a beloved component of meals across various cultures. The practice of creating mixed vegetable pickles involves not only the art of pickling itself but also an understanding of how different vegetables interact with the pickling brine and each other, resulting in a harmonious blend that is both nutritious and delicious. This section explores the intricacies of mixed vegetable pickles, including their preparation, cultural significance, and culinary uses, highlighting their unique position in the world of gastronomy.

The preparation of mixed vegetable pickles is a thoughtful process that begins with selecting fresh, high-quality vegetables. Common choices include cucumbers, carrots, cauliflower, onions, and bell peppers, though the possibilities are as vast as the vegetable kingdom itself. Each vegetable brings its own flavor, texture, and color to the mix, creating a pickle that is pleasing to the palate and the eye. The vegetables are typically cut into bite-sized pieces, ensuring they absorb the brine evenly and maintain a crisp texture.

The brine, a crucial component of any pickle, is a mixture of vinegar, water, salt, and often sugar, which acts as the preserving and flavoring agent. The acidity of the vinegar and the salinity of the salt work together to create an environment inhospitable to spoilage-causing microorganisms, ensuring the longevity of the pickles. Sugar, when used, balances the acidity, adding a delicate sweetness that complements the natural flavors of the vegetables. Spices and herbs, such as mustard seeds, peppercorns, dill, and garlic, are added to the brine to impart depth and complexity, making each bite a sensory experience.

The cultural significance of mixed vegetable pickles is profound, reflecting a universal desire to extend the enjoyment of the harvest and reduce food waste. Nearly every culinary tradition has its version of pickled vegetables, from South Asia's spicy achar to Italy's giardiniera. These pickles are more than just a preservation method; they reflect regional flavors, seasonal ingredients, and communal values. In many cultures, mixed vegetable pickles are associated with festivities and celebrations, serving as a symbol of abundance and the shared joy of eating.

Thanks to the variety of vegetables used, mixed vegetable pickles offer a plethora of nutritional benefits. They are high in vitamins, minerals, and antioxidants, providing a healthful boost to any meal. The fermentation process, prevalent in certain pickling types, can also introduce beneficial probiotics to the diet, supporting gut health. However, it's worth noting that the nutritional content can vary depending on the vegetables used and the pickling method, with some preparations being higher in sodium.

Culinarily, mixed vegetable pickles are incredibly versatile, adding a tangy, crunchy contrast to various dishes. They can be enjoyed as a refreshing appetizer, a zesty side dish, or a flavorful garnish, enhancing everything from sandwiches and salads to grilled meats and curries. The pickling liquid itself, infused with the essence of the vegetables and spices, can be used as a marinade or dressing, adding a burst of flavor to recipes. This versatility makes mixed vegetable pickles a staple in pantries worldwide, beloved for their ability to elevate the ordinary to the extraordinary.

In conclusion, mixed vegetable pickles are a culinary delight that transcends borders and traditions, offering a glimpse into the rich tapestry of global food preservation methods. Their preparation, rooted in the simple act of pickling, is elevated by the diversity of vegetables and flavors, resulting in a product that is as nutritious as it is delicious. The cultural significance of these pickles, coupled with their versatility in the kitchen, underscores their enduring popularity and importance in cuisines worldwide. As we continue to explore and celebrate the variety of pickled foods, mixed vegetable pickles stand out as a vibrant testament to the creativity, ingenuity, and shared heritage of cooks and food enthusiasts everywhere, preserving not just the bounty of the harvest but also the flavors and memories of the culinary traditions that bring us together.

CHAPTER IV

Fermenting Recipes

Sauerkraut with caraway seeds

Sauerkraut with caraway seeds is a classic dish that combines the tangy, fermented flavors of sauerkraut with the aromatic, earthy tones of caraway seeds, creating a harmony of tastes that is deeply rooted in culinary tradition. This combination not only enhances the complexity of sauerkraut's flavor but also brings a depth of cultural heritage and nutritional benefits to the table. The process of fermenting cabbage to make sauerkraut is an ancient practice, while the addition of caraway seeds is a tradition that varies by region, reflecting the adaptability and diverse culinary applications of this fermented food. This section explores the origins, preparation, and significance of sauerkraut with caraway seeds, shedding light on its enduring popularity and the role it plays in cuisines around the world.

The origin of sauerkraut dates back thousands of years, with various cultures around the world developing their own methods for fermenting cabbage. The addition of caraway seeds to a sauerkraut is a tradition that is particularly prevalent in Eastern European and German cuisines, where both sauerkraut and caraway seeds have been staple ingredients for centuries. Caraway seeds, with their distinctive flavor, were found to complement the tangy sharpness of sauerkraut, adding a layer of complexity to its taste and making it a versatile accompaniment to an array of dishes.

The process of making sauerkraut with caraway seeds begins with the selection of fresh, firm heads of cabbage. The cabbage is finely sliced and then mixed with salt to draw out its natural juices. Caraway seeds are added to the mixture, their quantities adjusted according to taste preference. The salted cabbage and caraway seeds are then tightly packed into a fermentation vessel, such as a crock or jar, and weighted down to submerge the cabbage in its liquid. This anaerobic environment is crucial for fermentation, allowing lactic acid bacteria to thrive and convert the cabbage's sugars into lactic acid. The result, after several weeks of fermentation, is sauerkraut with a tangy flavor, enhanced by the aromatic qualities of the caraway seeds.

The cultural significance of sauerkraut with caraway seeds is profoundly embedded in the culinary traditions of the regions where it is most popular. In Germany and Eastern Europe, it is not just a side dish but a symbol of comfort food, often served with sausages, pork, or other meats. The dish is also associated with festive occasions and family gatherings, representing a link to heritage and tradition. The practice of making sauerkraut has been passed down through generations, with the addition of caraway seeds becoming a distinctive mark of regional variations, showcasing the rich tapestry of culinary practices that define cultural identities.

Nutritionally, sauerkraut with caraway seeds is a powerhouse of health benefits. Sauerkraut is high in vitamins C and K, fiber, and probiotics, the beneficial bacteria that support gut health. Caraway seeds, meanwhile, are known for their digestive benefits, containing compounds that may help reduce bloating and gas. Together, they create a dish that is not only flavorful but also supportive of digestive wellness and overall health. This combination of health benefits and flavor has contributed to the growing popularity of sauerkraut with caraway seeds beyond its traditional roots, finding a place in the modern culinary landscape.

Culinarily, sauerkraut with caraway seeds is remarkably versatile. It can be enjoyed on its own as a tangy, flavorful side or used as an ingredient in salads, sandwiches, and casseroles. Its robust flavor complements rich, fatty meats, cutting through the heaviness and balancing the dish. The caraway seeds add a note of earthiness that pairs well with the natural tang of the sauerkraut, making it a distinctive and sought-after flavor profile in a variety of culinary contexts.

In conclusion, sauerkraut with caraway seeds is a dish that transcends mere food, embodying a rich history of culinary tradition, health benefits, and cultural significance. Its preparation, a testament to the art of fermentation, brings together the simple ingredients of cabbage and caraway seeds in a transformation that results in a complex, flavorful, and nutritious dish. As it continues to be embraced by new generations and incorporated into diverse culinary practices, sauerkraut with caraway seeds stands as a symbol of the enduring appeal of fermented foods and their ability to connect us to our past while providing for our nutritional and gastronomic needs in the present. Through this lens, sauerkraut with caraway seeds is not just a food but a cultural artifact, celebrating the simplicity, depth, and richness of culinary heritage across the globe.

Kimchi with Napa cabbage

Kimchi with Napa cabbage, a cornerstone of Korean cuisine, is a vibrant and spicy fermented dish that transcends its humble origins to embody the rich tapestry of flavors, textures, and traditions that define Korean food culture. This iconic dish, characterized by its pungent aroma and complex taste, is much more than a simple side dish; it symbolizes Korean identity, a staple at meals, and a testament to the art of fermentation. This section delves into the intricacies of making kimchi with Napa cabbage, exploring its cultural significance, preparation methods, and the nutritional benefits it offers, shedding light on why this fermented delicacy continues to captivate palates around the globe.

Making kimchi with Napa cabbage begins with the selection of fresh, crisp cabbage leaves, which serve as the canvas for the rich array of flavors imparted by various spices and seasonings. The cabbage is typically cut into pieces and then brined, a crucial step that softens the leaves and begins the fermentation process. The brine, usually a salty water solution, draws out moisture from the cabbage, creating an environment conducive to the growth of beneficial lactobacillus bacteria, which are instrumental in fermentation.

Once the cabbage has been sufficiently brined, it is rinsed and then mixed with a flavorful paste made from a blend of garlic, ginger, fish sauce, and, most importantly, gochugaru (Korean red pepper flakes). This spicy mixture is what gives kimchi its distinctive red hue and fiery taste. Additional ingredients such as radishes, green onions, and sometimes carrots or pear are added for extra crunch and flavor. Caraway seeds, while not traditionally used in kimchi, could be seen as an innovative addition by some, introducing an unexpected earthy note to the complex flavor profile of the dish.

The cultural significance of kimchi with Napa cabbage cannot be overstated. It is a dish steeped in history, with records of kimchi dating back to ancient times. Over the centuries, kimchi has evolved, with regional variations reflecting the diverse culinary landscape of Korea. It is a daily staple in Korean households, a source of pride, and a symbol of Korea's culinary heritage. The making of kimchi, especially in large quantities to last through the winter months, is a communal activity known as "kimjang," which reinforces social bonds and passes on traditional knowledge from generation to generation.

Nutritionally, kimchi with Napa cabbage is a powerhouse of health benefits. The fermentation process not only extends the shelf life of the cabbage but also enhances its nutritional value. Fermented foods which include kimchi are rich in probiotics, beneficial bacteria that encourage gut health and boost the immune system. Additionally,

Napa cabbage is packed with vitamins A and C, while the garlic and ginger in the seasoning paste offer anti-inflammatory and antioxidant properties. The capsaicin in gochugaru also contributes to the health benefits of kimchi, including improved metabolic rate and cardiovascular health.

Culinarily, kimchi with Napa cabbage is incredibly versatile. While it is often enjoyed as a side dish, it also plays a starring role in various Korean dishes, from kimchi stew (kimchi jjigae) and kimchi pancakes (kimchi jeon) to kimchi fried rice. Its unique taste as well as texture make it an excellent accompaniment to meats, adding a spicy, tangy kick that balances the richness of the dishes. It enhances flavors in recipes to an unparalleled depth, making it a beloved ingredient in Korean cuisine and fusion dishes worldwide.

In conclusion, kimchi with Napa cabbage is a culinary masterpiece that encapsulates the essence of Korean food culture. Its preparation is an art form that reflects centuries of tradition, while its taste and nutritional benefits underscore its continued relevance in a health-conscious world. The cultural significance of kimchi goes beyond its role as a food item; it symbolizes Korean heritage, community, and the enduring appeal of fermented foods. As kimchi continues to gain popularity worldwide, it acts as a bridge between cultures, inviting people to explore the depth and diversity of Korean cuisine. Through each jar of kimchi, we discover not only the flavors of Korea but also the stories, traditions, and communal spirit that make it such an integral part of Korean life.

Fermented pickles with dill

Fermented pickles with dill, a classic embodiment of the ancient art of fermentation, marry the crisp texture and fresh taste of cucumbers with dill's aromatic and slightly sweet flavor, all while being steeped in a tangy, probiotic-rich brine. This traditional method of preservation, predating refrigeration, harnesses the natural process of lacto-fermentation to not only extend the shelf life of cucumbers but also enhance their nutritional value and introduce a complexity of flavor that is both nuanced and deeply satisfying. Through the lens of fermented pickles with dill, we can explore the multifaceted dimensions of fermentation, its cultural significance, the meticulous preparation process, and the myriad health benefits it offers.

At the heart of fermented pickles with dill lies the process of lacto-fermentation, which relies on the natural existence of lactic acid bacteria in vegetables. When cucumbers are submerged in a saltwater solution, these beneficial bacteria begin converting the sugars in the cucumbers into lactic acid. This natural preservative prevents the growth of harmful bacteria, resulting in a safe, probiotic-rich food. Adding dill, alongside garlic, mustard seeds, and sometimes peppercorns or other spices, infuses the pickles with layers of flavor that develop and deepen over the fermentation period.

The cultural significance of fermented pickles with dill is profound, spanning various regions and eras. This humble pickle has roots in many Eastern European and Scandinavian countries, where the long, cold winters made preserving summer produce essential. Making these pickles became a yearly ritual, a means of ensuring a supply of vitamin-rich food throughout the seasons where fresh vegetables were scarce. The communal aspect of pickling, often involving family and neighbors, underscored the importance of these practices in cultural identity and culinary heritage, creating bonds and memories that were passed down through generations. Preparing fermented pickles with dill is both an art and a science, requiring attention to detail and an understanding of the fermentation process. It begins with selecting the right cucumbers—firm, fresh, and ideally of a variety known for pickling. These are cleaned and then packed into clean, sterilized jars along with fresh dill, and other flavorings. The saltwater brine, critical to fermentation, is poured over the cucumbers, making sure they are fully submerged. The jars are then covered with a cloth or a loose lid to allow gases produced during fermentation to escape while keeping out contaminants. At room temperature, the cucumbers transform into tangy, flavorful pickles for several days to a few weeks, with the brine becoming cloudy—a sign of active fermentation.

The nutritional benefits of fermented pickles with dill are significant. The lacto-fermentation process preserves the cucumbers, makes them more digestible, and increases their nutrient content. Rich in probiotics, these pickles support gut health, aiding in digestion and also the absorption of nutrients. Furthermore, cucumbers themselves are a good source of vitamins K and C, while dill provides additional antioxidants and minerals. This makes fermented pickles with dill a flavorful addition to meals and a healthful one.

Culinary uses for fermented pickles with dill are varied and abundant. Beyond their role as a crunchy, tangy accompaniment to sandwiches, burgers, and salads, they can be chopped and added to potato salads, used as a garnish for savory dishes, or simply enjoyed as a snack. The brine, too, is valuable, finding use in salad dressings, marinades, or as a flavorful liquid for cooking grains. The versatility and depth of flavor of these pickles make them a beloved ingredient in kitchens worldwide, celebrated for their ability to elevate the taste of a dish.

In conclusion, fermented pickles with dill are not just a culinary delight but also a link to our past, a nod to the ingenuity of traditional food preservation techniques.

They embody the connection between culture, health, and the pleasures of the table, offering a taste that is at once familiar and endlessly fascinating. Making and enjoying these pickles reminds us of the simplicity and wisdom inherent in traditional foods, encouraging a deeper appreciation for the natural processes that enrich our diets and lives. As we continue to explore and embrace fermented foods, fermented pickles with dill stand out as a testament to the enduring appeal of this ancient craft, inviting us to savor the flavors that bridge generations and cultures.

Fermented salsa with tomatoes and peppers

Fermented salsa with tomatoes and peppers is a culinary treasure that encapsulates fresh produce's vibrancy, enriched by fermentation's depth and complexity. This dynamic condiment, a fusion of ripe tomatoes, crisp peppers, and a symphony of spices, undergoes a transformation that elevates its flavors and boosts its nutritional profile. Through the ancient art of fermentation, simple ingredients meld into a tangy, slightly effervescent salsa, and brimming with probiotic benefits. This section delves into the craft of creating fermented salsa, exploring its origins, the meticulous process of fermentation, and its place in modern gastronomy.

The roots of salsa, and by extension fermented salsa, lie in the rich culinary traditions of Mesoamerica, where indigenous peoples cultivated tomatoes and peppers long before the arrival of Europeans. Salsa, meaning 'sauce' in Spanish, has been a staple in Latin American cuisine for centuries, evolving with European ingredients like onions and garlic. The practice of fermenting salsa is a nod to the pre-Columbian technique of preserving foods through lacto-fermentation, a method that not only extended the shelf life of harvests but also enhanced their flavors and digestibility.

Preparing fermented salsa begins with selecting high-quality, ripe tomatoes and crisp peppers—ingredients that form the heart of this dish. These are combined with onions, garlic, cilantro, and sometimes fruits like mango or pineapple for added sweetness. The key to fermentation lies in the brine, a saltwater solution that creates an anaerobic environment conducive to the development of lactic acid bacteria. These beneficial microbes are naturally present on the surface of vegetables, and when submerged in brine, they thrive, converting sugars into lactic acid. This process preserves the salsa, imparts a tangy flavor, and increases its probiotic content.

One of the critical aspects of fermenting salsa is maintaining the right conditions for fermentation to occur. The salsa must be kept at a stable temperature, away from direct sunlight, allowing the lactic acid bacteria to proliferate. As the fermentation progresses, the salsa undergoes a remarkable transformation—tomatoes and peppers soften slightly, their sharpness mellowed, and the overall flavor profile deepens, acquiring notes of complexity that raw salsa cannot replicate. This period of fermentation, which can last from a few days to a week or more, depending on personal taste and environmental factors, is what imbues the salsa with its unique character.

The cultural significance of fermented salsa with tomatoes and peppers is manifold, representing a confluence of tradition and innovation. It honors the ancestral food preservation practices while embracing contemporary interest in fermented foods, known for their health benefits and distinctive flavors. In this way, fermented salsa serves as a bridge between past and present, offering a familiar and novel taste. It is a testament to the enduring importance of fermentation in human diets, a practice that has grown in popularity as awareness of gut health and the microbiome expands.

Nutritionally, fermented salsa is a powerhouse. The tomatoes and peppers, already rich in vitamins C and A, antioxidants, and other phytonutrients, are enhanced by fermentation, increasing nutrient availability and introducing beneficial probiotics into the diet. These live microorganisms support digestive health, boost immunity, and may positively affect mental health. Fermented salsa, therefore, is not just a flavor enhancer but also a functional food that contributes to overall well-being.

Culinarily, fermented salsa with tomatoes and peppers is extraordinarily versatile. It can be used as a traditional salsa, accompanying chips, tacos, or grilled meats, adding a burst of flavor as well as complexity to every bite. However, its uses extend far beyond—incorporated into dressings, spread on sandwiches, or stirred into cooked dishes- bringing a tangy, umami-rich dimension that enhances the overall dish. The effervescence and depth of flavor of fermented salsa distinguish it from its non-fermented counterparts, making it a sought-after ingredient for those looking to elevate their culinary creations.

In conclusion, fermented salsa with tomatoes and peppers is a celebration of flavor, tradition, and the art of fermentation. It is a dish that connects us to ancient food preservation techniques while catering to contemporary tastes and nutritional needs. Making fermented salsa is both a craft and a journey that transforms simple ingredients into a complex, healthful condiment that captivates the senses. As we continue to explore and appreciate the world of fermented foods, fermented salsa stands out as a vibrant, flavorful testament to the creativity and ingenuity of cooks past and present, bridging cultures and generations through the shared language of food.

Fermented hot sauce

Fermented hot sauce is a testament to the profound transformation that can occur when the ancient art of fermentation meets the fiery heat of chili peppers. This culinary alchemy not only extends the shelf life of its ingredients but also enhances its flavors, creating a condiment that is far greater than the sum of its parts. Fermented hot sauce is both a bridge and a barrier between cultures, an expression of a culinary tradition that varies widely across the globe yet remains fundamentally tied to the universal human love for flavor and spice. This section delves into fermented hot sauce's origins, preparation, cultural significance, and culinary versatility, exploring how this fiery elixir captivates palates and cultures worldwide.

The process of creating fermented hot sauce begins with selecting chili peppers, the soul of the sauce. These can range from the milder jalapeños and serranos to the fiery habaneros and ghost peppers, depending on the desired heat level. Additional ingredients may be added to round out the flavors—garlic, onions, and sometimes fruits like mangoes or pineapples for sweetness, or carrots for earthiness. The choice of ingredients reflects personal preference, regional availability, and cultural influences, making each batch of fermented hot sauce a unique creation.

Salt is at the heart of the fermentation process, which is mixed with water to create a brine. The vegetables and fruits are submerged in this brine, creating an anaerobic environment where beneficial lactobacillus bacteria thrive. These bacteria ferment the sugars present in the ingredients, producing lactic acid which acts as a natural preservative. The fermentation process, which can last anywhere from a few days to several months, not only preserves the ingredients but also transforms their flavors, melding and deepening them into something complex and nuanced. The final step involves blending the fermented ingredients into a smooth or chunky sauce, depending on preference, and then bottling it for storage and use.

The cultural significance of fermented hot sauce is as varied as the ingredients that go into it. Across the globe, nearly every cuisine has its version of hot sauce, each reflecting its people's unique flavors and heat preferences. In the Caribbean, Scotch bonnet peppers are fermented with carrots and onions to create fiery sauces accompanying seafood and rice dishes. In Korea, gochujang is made from fermented chili paste, adding depth to soups and marinades. The tradition of fermenting hot sauce is rooted in the need to preserve the harvest but has grown into a culinary art form that celebrates the diversity of chili peppers and the creativity of those who transform them.

Nutritionally, fermented hot sauce offers more than just heat. The fermentation process expands the bioavailability of nutrients in the chili peppers, such as vitamin C, and introduces probiotics into the sauce, which can aid in digestion and support gut health. The capsaicin in chili peppers, responsible for their heat, has been shown to have anti-inflammatory and antioxidant properties, contributing to the health benefits of consuming fermented hot sauce in moderation.

Culinarily, fermented hot sauce is incredibly versatile. Its rich, tangy heat can elevate the simplest of meals, making it a staple in kitchens and on dining tables worldwide. It can be drizzled over tacos, stirred into soups and stews, or employed as a marinade for meats. The depth of flavor achieved through fermentation sets it apart from non-fermented hot sauces, making it a favorite among chefs and home cooks who appreciate its complexity and how it can enhance a dish without overpowering it.

In conclusion, fermented hot sauce is a celebration of flavor, a condiment that transcends cultural boundaries and unites food lovers in their appreciation for heat and depth in their dishes. Making it is both an art and a science, requiring patience and understanding the fermentation process. Its cultural significance reflects the global love for chili peppers and the desire to preserve their fiery flavor for year-round enjoyment. Nutritionally beneficial and culinarily versatile, fermented hot sauce is a testament to the power of fermentation to transform simple ingredients into something extraordinary. As we continue to explore and embrace the world of fermented foods, fermented hot sauce stands out as a vibrant example of how tradition and innovation can come together to create ancient and ever-new flavors.

Fermented beet kvass

Fermented beet kvass is a traditional Eastern European beverage that has garnered attention far beyond its origins for its distinctive flavor and reputed health benefits. This ruby-red elixir, made from fermented beets, salt, and water, is a testament to the simplicity and power of traditional fermentation processes. Its roots are profoundly embedded in the culture and dietary practices of the region, serving as a refreshing drink, a digestive tonic, and a culinary ingredient. This section delves into the history, preparation, cultural significance, and health benefits of fermented beet kvass, highlighting its unique position in the world of fermented foods and beverages.

The history of beet kvass dates back centuries, originating as a homemade remedy and a staple in the peasant diet of Eastern Europe. It was prized for its ability to quench thirst and its nutritional value, offering sustenance during the harsh winters when fresh vegetables were scarce. The fermentation process, a method of preservation employed long before the advent of refrigeration, allowed families to store their beet harvest in a liquid form that could be consumed throughout the year. With its deep, earthy flavor and gentle tang, Beet kvass became a beloved part of the culinary landscape, enjoyed by people of all ages.

The preparation of beet kvass is both simple and profound, requiring minimal ingredients but yielding a product rich in flavor and nutrients. The basic recipe involves chopping fresh beets into cubes, placing them in a jar or container with salt, and covering them with water. The salt not only seasons the kvass but also creates an environment conducive to lacto-fermentation, in which beneficial lactic acid bacteria thrive. These bacteria naturally present on the surface of the beets and in the air, initiate the fermentation process, metabolizing the sugars in the beets into lactic acid. Depending on the temperature and desired sourness, this fermentation process, which can take from a few days to over a week, transforms the simple mixture into kvass. The finished beverage is then strained, and the liquid is stored in the refrigerator, ready to be consumed.

The cultural significance of fermented beet kvass cannot be overstated. In Eastern European countries, it is more than just a drink; it symbolizes home, tradition, and connection to the land. Making kvass is often a family activity, with recipes and techniques passed down through generations. It is consumed as a beverage and used as a base for soups, such as the famous borscht, or as a medicinal tonic, believed to cleanse the blood and liver, improve digestion, and boost the immune system. The making and sharing of kvass embody the communal spirit and the value placed on natural, home-prepared foods in Eastern European culture.

The health benefits of fermented beet kvass are a vital reason for its enduring popularity. Beets are high in vitamins, minerals, as well as antioxidants, particularly betalains, which give beets their vibrant color and are known for their detoxifying properties. The fermentation process enhances these benefits, increasing the bioavailability of nutrients and introducing probiotics into the beverage, which promotes a healthy gut microbiome. Additionally, kvass is a hydrating and electrolyte-rich drink, making it the best choice for natural hydration. Compared to other fermented beverages like kombucha, its low sugar content makes it an appealing option for those seeking to lessen their sugar intake.

Culinarily, beet kvass offers a unique flavor profile that can enhance various dishes. Its earthy sweetness and subtle tang make it a versatile ingredient in dressings, marinades, and even cocktails, offering a novel way to introduce the flavors and benefits of fermentation into everyday meals. Its deep color also adds a visually striking element to dishes, making it a favorite among chefs and home cooks looking to experiment with traditional ingredients in new and creative ways.

In conclusion, fermented beet kvass is a remarkable beverage that bridges the gap between tradition and modern health trends, offering a glimpse into the culinary heritage of Eastern Europe while providing tangible health benefits. Its preparation, steeped in simplicity and tradition, results in a complex, nutrient-rich drink that has stood the test of time. The cultural significance of kvass, as a symbol of home and tradition, underscores the importance of fermented foods and beverages in our diet, not only for their health benefits but also for their ability to connect us to our cultural roots. As the interest in fermentation and traditional foods grows, fermented beet kvass stands out as a testament to the enduring appeal of simple, nourishing, and deliciously fermented beverages.

Fermented ginger carrots

Fermented ginger carrots are a vibrant and healthful addition to the world of fermented foods, combining the crisp sweetness of carrots with the spicy warmth of ginger in a tangy, probiotic-rich brine. This delightful concoction offers a unique flavor profile and boasts numerous health benefits, making it a popular choice among enthusiasts of traditional and health-conscious diets. The process of fermenting carrots with ginger is steeped in the ancient practice of lacto-fermentation, a method used for centuries to preserve food, enhance its nutritional value, and introduce beneficial bacteria to the diet. This section explores fermented ginger carrots' preparation, cultural significance, and nutritional benefits, highlighting their role in contemporary culinary practices and their contribution to a balanced diet.

The preparation of fermented ginger carrots begins with the selection of fresh, organic ingredients. The carrots are washed, peeled, and sliced into sticks or grated, depending on personal preference, while fresh ginger is peeled and finely chopped or grated. These ingredients are then mixed and packed into sterilized jars. A brine made from water and salt is poured over the mixture, ensuring the vegetables are completely submerged. The salt in the brine creates an environment where harmful bacteria cannot thrive but allows lactobacillus bacteria, naturally present on the surface of the vegetables, to ferment the sugars in the carrots and ginger. This fermentation process produces lactic acid, which acts as a natural preservative and gives fermented ginger carrots their characteristic tangy flavor.

The cultural significance of fermented vegetables, including ginger carrots, spans across many traditions and regions. Fermentation has been a cornerstone of human culinary practices for millennia, serving as a reliable method for preserving seasonal bounty and enhancing food's flavor and nutritional value. In many cultures, fermented foods are valued for their digestive health benefits and are often consumed alongside meals to aid in digestion. The inclusion of ginger, known for its medicinal properties in various traditional medicines, further enhances this ferment's cultural and health-related importance.

Nutritionally, fermented ginger carrots are a powerhouse of benefits. The fermentation process preserves the carrots and enhances their bioavailability, making it easier for the body to absorb the vitamins as well as minerals they contain. Carrots are rich in beta-carotene, an antioxidant that the body converts into vitamin A, which is crucial for healthy vision, skin, and immune function. Ginger adds its own array of health benefits, including anti-inflammatory and gastrointestinal relief. Additionally, the lactic acid bacteria in the ferment are probiotics that promote a healthy gut microbiome, aiding digestion and potentially improving immune function.

Culinarily, fermented ginger carrots offer a versatile and flavorful addition to various dishes. Their tangy crispness makes them an excellent condiment for sandwiches, salads, and grain bowls, refreshingly contrasting more decadent flavors. They can also be served as a side dish or appetizer, providing a probiotic boost to meals. The unique combination of carrots and ginger, with its balance of sweetness and spice, allows these fermented vegetables to complement both savory and sweet dishes, making them a favorite among chefs as well as home cooks exploring the realms of fermented foods.

In conclusion, fermented ginger carrots represent a delightful intersection of tradition, health, and flavor. The simple yet profound process of lacto-fermentation transforms these common ingredients into a condiment that is both nourishing and complex in taste. Beyond their culinary versatility, fermented ginger carrots carry the cultural heritage of fermentation practices, reminding us of the wisdom embedded in traditional methods of food preservation. As interest in fermented foods continues to grow, driven by their health benefits and unique flavors, fermented ginger carrots stand out as a testament to the enduring appeal of naturally fermented foods. Whether enjoyed for their probiotic properties, contribution to a balanced diet, or their vibrant taste, fermented ginger carrots offer a simple yet satisfying way to incorporate the art of fermentation into everyday meals.

Fermented apple chutney

Fermented apple chutney is a delightful fusion of sweet, tangy, and spicy flavors, marrying the natural sweetness of apples with a complex array of spices and the depth of flavor that only fermentation can bring. This condiment, a staple in many culinary traditions, is a testament to the versatility of apples as a fermentable fruit and the ingenuity of traditional preservation methods that enhance both the flavor and nutritional value of the ingredients. Through lacto-fermentation, fermented apple chutney becomes a probiotic-rich food that adds a flavorful accent to meals and contributes to gut health. This section delves into the preparation of fermented apple chutney, its cultural significance, and its place in the modern diet, exploring how this ancient preservation technique is finding new life in contemporary kitchens.

The preparation of fermented apple chutney begins with the selection of high-quality, ripe apples, which are the foundation of the chutney. These apples are typically peeled, cored, and chopped before being mixed with various ingredients, including onions, raisins, or other fruits, to add layers of flavor and texture. The spice blend used in apple chutney often features warming spices such as cinnamon, ginger, cloves, and nutmeg, which complement the sweetness of the apples and add an aromatic and palate-pleasing complexity.

To initiate the fermentation process, a brine is prepared, usually consisting of water and salt, and sometimes a starter culture is added to ensure a consistent and controlled fermentation. This mixture is combined with the apple mixture and packed into sterilized jars, ensuring that the fruit is submerged under the brine to create an anaerobic environment conducive to fermentation. The natural sugars in the apples and other ingredients are broken down by lactic acid bacteria for several days to a few weeks, producing lactic acid and transforming the chutney into a tangy, probiotic-rich condiment.

The cultural significance of apple chutney, and chutneys in general, is deeply rooted in the culinary traditions of South Asia, where chutneys of various types have been used for centuries to add flavor and zest to meals.

Fermenting chutney, including apple chutney, represents a convergence of culinary traditions and preservation methods, showcasing the adaptability of fermentation techniques across different ingredients and dishes. Fermented apple chutney, with its unique blend of flavors, is a modern take on these traditional chutneys, incorporating the principles of lacto-fermentation to enhance its health benefits and shelf life.

From a nutritional perspective, fermented apple chutney offers several benefits. The lacto-fermentation process not only preserves the apples and other ingredients but also enhances the bioavailability of nutrients, making them simpler for the body to absorb. Apples are a great resource of vitamin C, dietary fiber, and various antioxidants, while the spices commonly used in chutney have their own health-promoting properties, including anti-inflammatory and antimicrobial effects. Furthermore, the probiotics produced during fermentation can contribute to a healthy gut microbiome, aiding in digestion and potentially improving overall health.

Culinarily, fermented apple chutney is an incredibly versatile condiment that can be employed in many ways to enhance the flavor of dishes. It pairs well with cheese and crackers, making it an excellent charcuterie board addition. It can also be used as a topping for pork, chicken, or fish, adding a sweet as well as tangy contrast to the savory flavors of the meat. In vegetarian cuisine, fermented apple chutney can add depth and complexity to grain bowls, salads, and wraps. Its distinct flavor profile causes it to be a favorite among chefs as well as home cooks, who appreciate its ability to elevate the taste of a wide range of dishes.

In conclusion, fermented apple chutney is a rich and flavorful condiment embodying fermentation's art and science. Its preparation is a creative endeavor that blends the sweetness of apples with the warmth of spices, all transformed through the natural process of lacto-fermentation into a probiotic-rich food that is as healthful as it is delicious. The cultural significance of apple chutney, rooted in traditional chutney-making practices, is given new life through fermentation, highlighting the ongoing relevance of ancient food preservation methods in contemporary cuisine. As interest in fermented foods continues to grow, fermented apple chutney stands out as a testament to the enduring appeal of these foods, offering a compelling mix of flavors that enrich the culinary landscape and contribute to a healthy diet.

Fermented radish slices

Fermented radish slices represent a captivating blend of tradition, flavor, and nutritional prowess, illustrating the transformative power of fermentation on simple root vegetables. This process, rooted in ancient culinary practices, turns the crisp, peppery bite of radish into a tangy, flavorful, and probiotic-rich condiment that complements various dishes across various cuisines. Fermentation, a method revered for preserving food and enhancing its nutritional profile, imbues radishes with a complexity of taste and a host of health benefits, making fermented radish slices a cherished addition to the gastronomic world. This section delves into the intricacies of fermented radish slices, exploring their preparation, cultural significance, nutritional value, and versatility in culinary applications.

Preparing fermented radish slices begins with selecting fresh, firm radishes, preferably those that are organically grown, to ensure the presence of beneficial bacteria on their skins. These radishes are washed, trimmed, and sliced, with the thickness of the slices varying according to personal preference, though thinner slices tend to ferment more quickly. The fundamental aspect of fermenting radish slices lies in creating a brine, typically a solution of water and salt, which serves as the medium for fermentation. Salt plays a crucial role, inhibiting the growth of undesirable microorganisms while promoting the proliferation of lactobacillus bacteria, responsible for the fermentation process. These beneficial bacteria metabolize the natural sugars present in the radish, producing lactic acid, which acts as a natural preservative and gives fermented radish slices their characteristic tangy flavor.

The cultural significance of fermented radishes is deeply embedded in the culinary traditions of many countries, reflecting the global appreciation for fermented foods. In Korean cuisine, radish is a critical ingredient in kimchi, showcasing its versatility and importance. Similarly, Japanese, Chinese, and Eastern European cuisines have their versions of fermented radish, each with unique flavors and preparation methods that highlight the adaptability of this humble vegetable to different taste preferences and dietary practices. Fermenting radishes is not just about preserving food; it is a celebration of cultural heritage, a way to maintain a connection to ancestral roots and traditional food preparation techniques.

Nutritionally, fermented radish slices offer a plethora of benefits. The fermentation process promotes the bioavailability of nutrients, making it easier for the body to absorb the vitamins and minerals present in radishes. Rich in vitamin C, radishes also contain essential minerals such as potassium and calcium, contributing to overall health and well-being. Furthermore, the presence of dietary fiber in radishes supports digestive health. The lactic acid bacteria that thrive during fermentation are probiotics, known for their beneficial effects on the gut microbiome, aiding in digestion, boosting the immune system, and potentially mitigating the risk of certain chronic diseases.

Culinarily, fermented radish slices are incredibly versatile, adding depth and complexity to various dishes. Their crisp texture and tangy flavor make them an excellent accompaniment to rich, fatty meats, cutting through the heaviness with a refreshing zest. They can be incorporated into salads for an added punch of flavor, used as a garnish on soups and stews, or as part of a charcuterie board, complementing cheeses and cured meats. The brine from fermented radishes can also be used in salad dressings or as a base for marinades, infusing dishes with its probiotic-rich, tangy essence. This versatility underscores the culinary potential of fermented radish slices, allowing them to transcend cultural and dietary boundaries.

In conclusion, fermented radish slices stand as a testament to the enduring appeal of fermentation as a method of food preservation and enhancement. Through the simple yet profound process of lacto-fermentation, radishes are transformed from a common root vegetable into a probiotic-rich, flavorful condiment that spans cultures and cuisines. Preparing fermented radish slices reflects a harmonious blend of science and tradition, where the microbial world meets culinary art to create something truly extraordinary. Their nutritional benefits and culinary versatility make fermented radish slices a valuable addition to any diet, offering a delicious way to enjoy the healthful advantages of fermented foods. As we continue to explore and embrace the rich diversity of fermented foods, fermented radish slices act as a vibrant reminder of the beauty as well as simplicity inherent in traditional food practices, inviting us to rediscover the flavors and wisdom of our culinary heritage.

CHAPTER V

Combining Pickling and Fermenting

Pickle-fermented vegetables

Pickle-fermented vegetables embody a timeless culinary tradition that marries the art of preservation with the science of fermentation, creating a harmony of flavors that are as diverse as they are delicious. This ancient technique, which has spanned cultures and millennia, not only extends the shelf life of seasonal produce but also enhances its nutritional profile, introducing a complex array of tastes and textures that have become integral to global cuisines. The process of pickle fermentation transforms ordinary vegetables into tangy, probiotic-rich delicacies, revered not only for their health benefits but also for their ability to elevate the culinary experience. This section explores the multifaceted world of pickle-fermented vegetables, delving into their preparation methods, cultural significance, nutritional value, and versatility in cooking.

Preparing pickle-fermented vegetables is a testament to the ingenuity of traditional food preservation methods. It begins with selecting fresh, high-quality vegetables — cucumbers, carrots, radishes, and cabbage are just a few popular choices. These vegetables are then cleaned and prepared, often sliced or left whole, depending on the desired outcome. The heart of the fermentation process lies in creating a brine, a solution of water and salt, to which various seasonings and spices may be added for flavor. This brine acts as both a preservative and a catalyst for fermentation, inhibiting the development of harmful bacteria while also promoting the proliferation of beneficial lactobacillus bacteria. These bacteria, naturally present on the surface of the vegetables, commence the fermentation process, converting sugars into lactic acid, which imparts the characteristic tangy flavor of pickle-fermented vegetables.

The cultural significance of pickle-fermented vegetables is profound, reflecting the human desire to harness nature's bounty for sustenance and pleasure. Across the globe, from the kimchi of Korea to the sauerkraut of Germany, fermented vegetables hold a place of honor in the culinary traditions of numerous societies. These foods are not merely about preservation; they represent a celebration of seasonal cycles, a connection to the land, and a reverence for the generations of knowledge that have culminated in their creation. Fermentation festivals and traditional communal preparations, such as kimjang in Korea, underscore the role of pickle-fermented vegetables in fostering community bonds and cultural identity.

Nutritionally, pickle-fermented vegetables offer many benefits, making them a valuable addition to a health-conscious diet. The fermentation process not only preserves the vegetables but also enhances their digestibility and increases the availability of vitamins and minerals. Rich in probiotics, fermented vegetables support gut health, contributing to a balanced microbiome, improved digestion, and a strengthened immune system. Moreover, the lactic acid produced during fermentation acts as a natural preservative, eliminating the need for artificial additives and ensuring the wholesomeness of the final product.

Culinarily, pickle-fermented vegetables are incredibly versatile, capable of transforming the simplest of meals into something extraordinary. They can be enjoyed as a tangy, crunchy side dish, adding depth and contrast to rich and savory flavors. Incorporated into salads, sandwiches, and wraps, they introduce a refreshing zest that balances the palate. In cooking, fermented vegetables can be used as a critical ingredient in soups, stews, and sauces, lending their unique flavors to various dishes. The brine itself, imbued with the essence of the fermented vegetables and spices, can be utilized as a flavorful base for marinades, dressings, or even as a cocktail mixer, showcasing the creative potential of pickle fermentation in the culinary arts.

In conclusion, pickle-fermented vegetables stand at the crossroads of tradition and innovation, offering a vibrant testament to the enduring appeal of fermentation as both a science and an art. Through the simple act of submerging vegetables in brine, a world of flavors is unlocked, reflecting the rich tapestry of global food cultures and the shared human experience of transforming nature's gifts into nourishing, delightful foods. The preparation of pickle-fermented vegetables is a practice steeped in history, yet it continues to evolve, inviting modern interpretations and techniques that respect the past while embracing the future. Their cultural significance extends beyond the plate, symbolizing the continuity of culinary heritage and the importance of sustainable food practices. Nutritionally beneficial and culinarily adaptable, pickle-fermented vegetables enrich our diets and lives, offering a delicious way to connect with the natural world, our communities, and the generations that have paved the way for these treasured foods to grace our tables. As we continue to explore the depths of fermented cuisine, pickle-fermented vegetables remind us of the beauty in preservation, the joy in creation, and the endless possibilities that await in the simple act of combining salt, water, vegetables, and time.

Fermented pickled fruits

Fermented pickled fruits, an exquisite confluence of the ancient practices of pickling and fermentation, stand as a testament to humanity's ingenuity in food preservation and flavor enhancement. This culinary tradition, which spans cultures and epochs, not only prolongs the shelf life of seasonal bounty but also elevates the taste and nutritional profile of fruits, transforming them into tangy, probiotic-rich delicacies. By harnessing the natural process of lacto-fermentation, fermented pickled fruits offer a complex array of flavors and textures, making them a cherished ingredient in many culinary contexts. This section delves into the intricate world of fermented pickled fruits, exploring their preparation methods, their cultural significance, their health benefits, and their versatility in the culinary arts.

Preparing fermented pickled fruits begins with selecting high-quality, ripe fruits, which are then cleaned and prepared according to the desired outcome. Popular choices include apples, pears, cherries, and peaches, though virtually any fruit can be fermented, each offering its unique flavor profile. The fruits may be left whole, sliced, or chopped, then submerged in a brine made from water and salt, occasionally with the addition of a sweetener such as honey or sugar to balance the acidity. Spices and herbs may also be introduced to the mix, such as cinnamon, cloves, vanilla, or mint, to infuse the fruits with additional layers of flavor. The brine creates an anaerobic environment conducive to the growth of lactobacillus bacteria, which naturally occur on the skin of fruits. These bacteria initiate the fermentation process, metabolizing the natural sugars in the fruit into lactic acid, thereby preserving the fruit and imbuing it with a distinctive tangy taste.

The cultural significance of fermented pickled fruits is deeply rooted in the global heritage of food preservation. Throughout history, in the absence of modern refrigeration, cultures worldwide developed methods to extend the life of their food resources. Fermentation emerged as a critical technique, with fruits being among the diverse array of foods preserved through this method. In regions where fruit was abundant but the growing season short, fermenting fruit allowed communities to enjoy their flavors year-round, celebrating the seasons' bounties even in times of scarcity. These traditions have been passed down through generations, with fermented pickled fruits remaining a symbol of culinary resourcefulness and a connection to the past.

Nutritionally, fermented pickled fruits offer many health benefits, making them valuable to a balanced diet. The lacto-fermentation process not only preserves the fruit but also enhances its digestibility and increases the availability of vitamins and minerals. The probiotics generated during fermentation benefit gut health, aiding digestion and contributing to a robust microbiome. Moreover, the lactic acid produced acts as a natural preservative, eliminating the need for artificial additives and ensuring the wholesomeness of the final product.

Culinarily, fermented pickled fruits are exceptionally versatile, finding their place in various dishes and preparations. They can be enjoyed as a tangy, flavorful snack on their own or used as an ingredient to add depth and complexity to sweet and savory dishes. In salads, they introduce a refreshing contrast to leafy greens; in desserts, they offer a tangy counterpoint to sweetness; and in meat dishes, they provide a burst of acidity that balances rich flavors. Additionally, the brine from fermented pickled fruits, infused with the essence of the fruits and spices, can be used in dressings, marinades, or even cocktails, showcasing the creative potential of this ancient preservation method in modern culinary practices.

In conclusion, fermented pickled fruits embody the harmony between tradition and innovation, offering a window into the ancient world of food preservation while continuing to inspire contemporary cuisine. Their preparation is a celebration of nature's abundance, a process that extends the enjoyment of seasonal fruits and enhances their flavor and health benefits. The cultural significance of fermented pickled fruits reflects the shared human experience of adapting to and thriving within our environments, preserving the wisdom of the past while nourishing the present. Nutritionally beneficial and culinarily adaptable, fermented pickled fruits enrich our diets and palates, inviting us to explore the depths of flavor that fermentation can unlock. As we continue to rediscover and embrace the traditions of fermenting and pickling, fermented pickled fruits stand as a vibrant testament to the enduring appeal of these practices, bridging cultures, generations, and tastes in the universal language of food.

Pickle-fermented relishes

Pickle-fermented relishes stand as a testament to the intricate dance between the art of preservation and the science of fermentation, a culinary practice that stretches back to ancient times. This unique method of preparation not only extends the shelf life of seasonal produce but also enhances its flavors and nutritional profile, imbuing it with a complexity and depth that is both tangy and rich. Across cultures and cuisines, pickle-fermented relishes are celebrated as condiments and essential components of gastronomy, capable of transforming ordinary dishes into extraordinary culinary experiences. This section delves into the preparation, cultural significance, nutritional value, and culinary versatility of pickle- fermented relishes, offering insights into their enduring popularity and their role in modern culinary practices.

The preparation of pickle-fermented relishes begins with selecting fresh vegetables and sometimes fruits, which are then finely chopped or grated to create a base for the relish. Common ingredients include cucumbers, onions, bell peppers, and carrots, though the variety of produce used can vary widely depending on regional preferences and seasonal availability. To this mix, spices and seasonings are added, which might range from mustard seeds and turmeric to dill and garlic, each contributing to the unique flavor profile of the relish. The critical component of pickle fermentation is the brine, a solution of water and salt, which may also include vinegar for additional acidity. This brine creates an environment conducive to lacto-fermentation, wherein beneficial bacteria naturally present on the surface of the vegetables begin to convert sugars into lactic acid, preserving the relish and infusing it with a distinctive tangy flavor.

The cultural significance of pickle-fermented relishes is deeply rooted in the history of food preservation, reflecting humanity's enduring relationship with fermentation as a means to safeguard and savor the bounty of the harvest. In many cultures, relishes are not just culinary additives but symbols of tradition and heritage, passed down through generations. They are integral to celebrations and everyday meals alike, embodying the flavors of home and the creativity of those who prepare them. From the chutneys of India to the chow-chow of the American South, pickle-fermented relishes represent a global tapestry of culinary ingenuity, each variety telling a story of cultural identity and adaptation.

Nutritionally, pickle-fermented relishes offer a wealth of benefits, thanks in large part to the process of lacto-fermentation. This method preserves the ingredients, makes them more digestible, and enhances their nutritional content. Fermented relishes are rich in probiotics, beneficial bacteria that encourage gut health and support the immune system. Additionally, the vegetables used in these relishes are sources of essential vitamins and minerals, while the spices can offer anti-inflammatory and antioxidant properties. Consuming pickle-fermented relishes can thus contribute to a balanced diet, offering a delicious way to incorporate fermented foods into one's culinary repertoire.

Culinarily, pickle-fermented relishes are marvelously versatile and capable of elevating a wide range of dishes with their zesty and complex flavors. They can be used as condiments, providing a tangy contrast to savory dishes such as grilled meats, sandwiches, and burgers. Salads and side dishes add texture and a burst of flavor that can refresh and revitalize the palate. Moreover, their rich taste profile allows them to be incorporated into sauces and dressings, infusing meals with the layered and fermented essence that is characteristic of pickle-fermented foods. The versatility of pickle-fermented relishes underscores their importance in culinary traditions worldwide, serving as a testament to their adaptability and enduring appeal.

In conclusion, pickle-fermented relishes embody the confluence of preservation, flavor, and nutrition, offering a glimpse into the world of fermented foods that is as diverse as it is delicious. Their preparation, steeped in the ancient art of lacto-fermentation, celebrates tradition and innovation, allowing for the creation of tangy, rich, and probiotic relishes. Across cultures, pickle-fermented relishes hold a place of significance, cherished for their ability to capture the essence of seasons past and present them anew in each bite. Nutritionally valuable and culinarily versatile, these relishes are more than mere condiments; they are vibrant expressions of culinary heritage, enhancing dishes with their depth of flavor and contributing to a healthful diet. As we continue to explore and embrace the complexities of fermented foods, pickle-fermented relishes stand as a flavorful reminder of the transformative power of fermentation, inviting us to savor the artistry and science that make them such a cherished part of our global culinary landscape.

Tips for successful combination recipes

Creating successful combination recipes in the realm of pickling and fermenting is an art that marries the intricate dance of flavors and textures with the scientific precision of the fermentation process. This culinary pursuit, which extends beyond mere preservation to enhancing food, demands a deep understanding of the ingredients, the fermentation environment, and the desired flavor outcomes. As more culinary enthusiasts explore the boundless possibilities within pickling and fermenting, a set of guiding principles emerges, offering a roadmap to crafting dishes that are not only safe and nutritious but also rich in complexity and taste. This section outlines essential tips for achieving success in the combined art of pickling and fermenting, emphasizing the importance of ingredient selection, the balance of flavors, the control of fermentation conditions, and the art of experimentation.

The first step toward successful combination recipes in pickling and fermenting begins with meticulous ingredient selection. High-quality, fresh ingredients free from blemishes and signs of spoilage are crucial, as the fermentation process can amplify any imperfections, affecting the final product's flavor and safety. When combining ingredients, consider their individual fermenting times and how they complement each other. For instance, combining vegetables with similar densities ensures an even fermentation process, resulting in a harmonious blend of flavors and textures.

Understanding and balancing flavors is paramount in creating combination recipes that are both delightful and harmonious. The complexity of fermented flavors—sour, salty, umami, and sometimes sweet—requires carefully considering how different ingredients and seasonings will interact over the fermentation period. Adding aromatic herbs, spices, or additional flavorings can enhance the primary ingredients, but it's essential to use them judiciously to avoid overwhelming the natural flavors of the vegetables or fruits being fermented. The key is to aim for a balance that respects the individuality of each ingredient while creating a cohesive flavor profile.

Controlling the fermentation environment is another critical aspect of successful combination recipes. The temperature, salinity of the brine, and fermentation duration can significantly impact the final product's safety, texture, and taste. Keeping the fermentation vessel in a cool, dark place and ensuring the ingredients are fully submerged in the brine are essential yet vital steps to prevent unwanted bacterial growth and ensure a successful fermentation process. Monitoring the pH and using weights to submerge ingredients can help maintain an ideal environment for the beneficial bacteria to thrive.

Experimentation and adaptation are at the heart of innovative pickling and fermenting. The willingness to experiment with different combinations of ingredients and seasonings can lead to delightful discoveries and unique flavors. However, experimentation should always be guided by an understanding of the principles of safe fermentation practices to make sure that the final product is delicious and safe to consume. Keeping detailed notes on ingredient ratios, fermentation conditions, and flavor outcomes can provide valuable insights for refining recipes over time.

Patience is a virtue in the world of pickling and fermenting. Unlike cooking methods that offer immediate results, fermentation is a slow process that unfolds over days, weeks, or even months. The development of flavors and textures during this time is a natural progression that cannot be rushed. Allowing the fermentation to proceed at its own pace, checking periodically for signs of progress or any issues, is part of the journey toward creating successful combination recipes.

Understanding the cultural origins and traditions behind the fermentation practices can enrich the pickling and fermenting experience. Many fermented foods have deep cultural roots, with specific techniques and flavor profiles passed down through generations. Respecting these traditions while incorporating them into combination recipes can add depth and authenticity to the final product, bridging the gap between traditional and innovative culinary practices.

Presentation and serving suggestions can also enhance the appeal of pickled and fermented combination recipes.

The vibrant colors and textures of fermented foods make them a culinary delight and a visual one. Serving these creations as part of a carefully curated dish or alongside complementary flavors can elevate the dining experience, showcasing the beauty and complexity of fermented foods.

In conclusion, creating successful combination recipes in pickling and fermenting is a multifaceted endeavor that blends art, science, tradition, and innovation. It demands a thoughtful approach to ingredient selection, flavor balancing, and environmental control, underpinned by a spirit of experimentation and patience. By adhering to these principles and respecting the rich cultural heritage of fermentation, culinary enthusiasts can explore new horizons of taste and texture, crafting fermented foods that are not only nutritious and safe but also a testament to the endless possibilities of flavor that await in the magical process of fermentation.

CHAPTER VI

Beyond the Basics: Advanced Techniques and Recipes

Using fermentation crocks

Fermentation crocks, the venerable vessels of traditional food preservation, are a testament to the enduring craft of fermenting foods. Rooted in history yet embraced by the modern culinary world, these crocks are explicitly designed for fermenting vegetables and fruits, allowing the natural process of lacto-fermentation to unfold in an optimal environment. This section delves into the use of fermentation crocks, exploring their design, benefits, and their crucial role in the fermentation process, while providing guidance on how to use them to achieve successful fermentation effectively.

Fermentation crocks' design is simple and ingenious, embodying centuries of culinary tradition. Typically made of stoneware or ceramic, these crocks provide an anaerobic environment essential for fermentation, wherein vegetables are submerged under a brine without oxygen. This environment is critical for promoting the growth of beneficial lactobacillus bacteria, which ferment the sugars in the vegetables, producing lactic acid and preserving the food. Many fermentation crocks come with a water-sealed lid or airlock system, designed to let gases escape while preventing air from entering, further ensuring the anaerobic conditions necessary for successful fermentation.

The benefits of using fermentation crocks are manifold. Firstly, the material from which these crocks are made helps maintain a stable temperature throughout the fermentation process, which is crucial for the consistent growth of lactobacillus bacteria. The thick walls of the crock insulate the fermenting food, buffering it against sudden temperature changes that could disrupt the fermentation process. Furthermore, using fermentation crocks minimizes the risk of contamination by harmful bacteria or molds, thanks to their design which keeps the ferment fully submerged under the brine and away from oxygen. Lastly, the aesthetic appeal of fermentation crocks, with their rustic charm, adds a visual element to the art of fermentation, celebrating the beauty of this age-old culinary practice.

Successfully using fermentation crocks involves several key steps, starting with preparing the vegetables or fruits to be fermented. This includes washing the produce thoroughly and then cutting or shredding it as desired.

The produce is then mixed with salt, either by sprinkling salt directly onto it and massaging it in, which draws out water from the vegetables and creates a natural brine, or by preparing a separate saltwater brine in which the produce will be submerged. The salt concentration is crucial, as it inhibits the growth of harmful bacteria while allowing lactobacillus bacteria to thrive.

Once the vegetables are prepared and placed in the crock, it is essential to ensure that they are fully submerged under the brine. This can be achieved by placing a weight on top of the vegetables, such as a ceramic or glass weight designed for this purpose, or even a clean, boiled rock. The crock is then covered with its lid or airlock system, and fermentation begins. The length of fermentation can vary, from a few days to several weeks or even longer, depending on the temperature, the type of vegetables, and the desired taste as well as texture of the final product.

Monitoring the fermentation process is an integral part of using fermentation crocks effectively. This involves checking the crock periodically to ensure that the vegetables remain submerged and that no mold or unwanted bacteria have developed on the brine's surface. Any scum that forms can usually be skimmed off without affecting the ferment. Tasting the ferment at different stages can help determine when it has reached the desired level of sourness and is ready to be transferred to the refrigerator or other cool storage, which slows down the fermentation process and preserves the fermented food for more extended periods.

In conclusion, fermentation crocks are invaluable tools for anyone exploring the world of fermented foods. Their design, rooted in tradition but perfect for modern kitchens, provides the ideal environment for successful fermentation, offering both practical and aesthetic benefits. By following the key steps of preparation, submerging, covering, and monitoring, culinary enthusiasts can harness the power of fermentation to create nutritious, flavorful, and probiotic-rich foods. The use of fermentation crocks connects us to a rich culinary heritage and opens up new opportunities for creativity and experimentation in the kitchen, allowing us to discover the delicious potential of fermented foods.

Troubleshooting common issues in pickling and fermenting

Pickling and fermenting are ancient culinary practices revered for preserving food and enhancing its flavors and nutritional profile. Despite their simplicity, these methods can sometimes present challenges, even to the experienced fermenter or pickler. Troubleshooting common issues in pickling and fermenting is essential to ensure the final product's safety, quality, and taste. This section explores challenges that might arise during these processes, offering insights and solutions to help novices and seasoned practitioners achieve successful outcomes.

One common issue faced in the world of fermentation is the development of mold. Mold can appear on the surface of fermenting foods when they are exposed to air, as fermentation is an anaerobic process requiring the absence of oxygen. To prevent mold growth, ensuring that the vegetables or fruits are fully submerged under the brine is crucial. Using weights or fermentation stones can help keep the produce below the surface. If mold does appear, it's generally safe to remove the moldy parts along with an inch of the ferment below it, as the lactic acid present in the brine typically prevents the mold from penetrating deeply into the ferment.

Another challenge is soft or mushy pickles, which can result from enzymes naturally present in vegetables breaking down their structure. To combat this, many picklers add leaves high in tannins, such as grape, oak, or horseradish leaves, to the pickling jar, as tannins help maintain the pickles' crispness. Ensuring the use of fresh, firm vegetables and the correct concentration of salt in the brine can also help preserve the desired texture.

Kahm yeast is another common concern, a thin, white, filmy layer that sometimes forms on the surface of fermenting vegetables. While it is not harmful, its presence can indicate that the ferment is not acidic enough to prevent unwanted bacteria growth, potentially affecting the taste and safety of the ferment. Ensuring a correct seal on the fermentation vessel to limit oxygen exposure and checking that the vegetables are fully submerged can help prevent kahm yeast. If it does form, skimming it off the surface and ensuring the remaining ferment is still submerged under the brine should resolve the issue.

Unpleasant odors can also arise during fermentation, causing concern. While fermentation can produce strong smells, particularly in the early stages, these should not be foul or rotten. Unpleasant odors may indicate contamination or spoilage. Ensuring cleanliness in all steps of the preparation and fermentation process, from the vessels used to the hands and tools involved, is crucial in preventing this issue. If a ferment smells bad, it's safer to discard it and start again, as consuming spoiled fermented foods can pose health risks.

Failure to ferment is another issue that can occur, resulting in a lack of the expected tangy flavor or the production of carbon dioxide bubbles. This can be due to several factors, including too much salt in the brine, temperatures that are too low for fermentation to occur effectively, or the use of chlorinated water, which can inhibit the growth of beneficial bacteria. Adjusting the salt concentration, ensuring the ferment is kept at a suitable temperature, and using filtered or dechlorinated water can help encourage successful fermentation.

Discoloration of the pickles or brine can sometimes occur during pickling. This can be caused by minerals in the water, reactions with metal lids or utensils, or the natural pigments in the vegetables. Using distilled or filtered water, non-reactive containers and lids, and ensuring that the vegetables are fresh can help maintain the desired appearance of pickles.

Lastly, developing off-flavors in pickled or fermented products can be disheartening. This issue may stem from several sources, including the quality of ingredients, contamination, or incorrect proportions of spices and seasonings. Using high-quality, fresh produce and spices, following trusted recipes, and maintaining strict hygiene practices throughout the process can help guarantee that the final product has the desired flavors.

In conclusion, while pickling and fermenting are rewarding methods of food preservation with a rich history, they can sometimes present challenges that need to be addressed to ensure the final product's success. Understanding the common issues that can arise and knowing how to troubleshoot them is essential for anyone engaged in these practices. By ensuring cleanliness, monitoring the environment in which foods are fermented or pickled, and paying close attention to the ingredients and conditions, enthusiasts can continue to enjoy the delicious as well as healthful benefits of pickled and fermented foods. With patience and practice, overcoming these challenges can result in a more profound appreciation for the art and science of fermentation and pickling, enriching one's culinary adventures.

Experimenting with flavors and ingredients

Experimenting with flavors and ingredients in pickling and fermenting is an exciting journey through culinary creativity, offering endless possibilities to transform ordinary foods into extraordinary tastes and textures. This ancient practice, deeply rooted in cultures around the world, serves as a method of preservation and a canvas for innovation. The adventurous cook who delves into the world of pickling and fermenting can unlock complex flavors, enhance nutritional value, and introduce a unique character to dishes that delight and surprise the palate. This section explores the vast potential for experimentation within the realms of pickling and fermenting, discussing the importance of understanding foundational techniques, the exploration of diverse ingredients, the role of spices and seasonings, and the benefits of embracing creativity and patience in the process.

Understanding foundational techniques is crucial for successful experimentation in pickling and fermenting. These techniques, which have been honed over centuries, provide a necessary framework for ensuring safety and achieving desired outcomes. Fermentation relies on controlling environmental factors to encourage the growth of beneficial bacteria, yeast, or molds while pickling often involves submerging foods in vinegar or saltwater brine. Mastery of these techniques allows for informed experimentation, ensuring that adjustments to ingredients or processes do not compromise the integrity or safety of the final product. Knowledge of the principles behind lacto-fermentation, vinegar pickling, and other methods empowers the cook to venture into creative experimentation confidently.

Exploring diverse ingredients is at the heart of experimenting with flavors in pickling and fermenting. Beyond traditional cucumbers, cabbages, and carrots, a world of vegetables, fruits, and even proteins awaits. Unusual or underutilized produce, such as watermelon radishes, green strawberries, or fiddlehead ferns, can offer unique flavors and textures when pickled or fermented. Fruits, often overlooked in fermentation, can create delightful, tangy condiments or beverages with a depth of flavor. Experimenting with proteins, like fermenting fish or pickling eggs, extends the boundaries of traditional practices, introducing new tastes and culinary applications. Each ingredient brings its own set of characteristics to the process, inviting exploration and discovery.

The role of spices and seasonings in pickling and fermenting cannot be overstated. They are the alchemists' tools, transforming the base ingredients into complex flavor profiles. Classic combinations, such as dill and garlic in cucumber pickles or chili and garlic in kimchi, serve as starting points for further experimentation. Incorporating less traditional spices and herbs, such as star anise, juniper berries, or lemon verbena, can introduce unexpected aromas and tastes. Blending cultural flavor profiles, such as adding Mexican oregano to Korean-style fermented vegetables, can result in fusion creations that are both innovative and respectful of the original traditions. Experimentation with spices and seasonings offers an opportunity to personalize pickles and ferments, tailoring them to individual preferences and culinary inspirations.

Embracing creativity and patience is fundamental to the experimentation process. The art of pickling and fermenting is as much about the journey as it is about the destination. Each batch is an opportunity to learn, adjust, and refine. Creative experimentation may lead to unexpected results, some of which may redefine personal tastes or culinary practices. It requires an openness to failure and a willingness to embrace the unexpected. Patience is equally important, as fermentation is a slow process, governed by the natural rhythms of microbial activity. Allowing time for flavors to develop fully can yield remarkable results, rewarding the patient cook with depth and complexity that cannot be rushed.

In conclusion, experimenting with flavors and ingredients in pickling and fermenting opens up a world of culinary possibilities. It challenges conventional notions of taste, texture, and food preservation, inviting cooks to explore new territories and create signature flavors. Understanding foundational techniques provides a solid basis for this exploration, ensuring that experiments are safe and successful. Diverse ingredients offer a palette of flavors and textures, while spices and seasonings act as catalysts for transformation. Embracing creativity and patience allows for fully realizing the potential in each jar of pickles or ferment. This journey of discovery not only enriches the culinary repertoire but also deepens the appreciation for the ancient art of pickling and fermenting, celebrating its continued relevance and endless capacity for innovation.

Advanced pickling and fermenting recipes

Advanced pickling and fermenting recipes represent the pinnacle of culinary artistry in the realm of preservation, allowing enthusiasts to explore complex flavors, textures, and techniques that transcend traditional boundaries. These recipes are not merely about extending the shelf life of food but are a celebration of culture, science, and gastronomy, offering a deep dive into the nuanced world of fermented and pickled delicacies. From intricate flavor combinations to sophisticated methods, advanced pickling and fermenting challenge conventional practices, inviting cooks to embark on a journey of discovery and mastery. This section delves into the sophisticated world of advanced pickling and fermenting recipes, exploring their complexity, the importance of precision and patience, and their impact on culinary traditions and contemporary cuisine.

Advanced pickling and fermenting recipes often involve complex flavor combinations that require a discerning palate and a creative approach. These recipes may combine unusual or unexpected ingredients to create new taste experiences. For instance, a recipe might pair beets' earthy sweetness with ginger's aromatic sharpness in a fermented relish, or blend the tropical notes of pineapple with fiery habanero peppers in a hot sauce. Such combinations demand not only an understanding of individual ingredients but also an appreciation of how flavors evolve over time through fermentation or pickling, creating layers of taste that are both rich and nuanced.

Precision and patience are paramount in the execution of advanced recipes. Unlike simple pickles or straightforward ferments, advanced recipes may require careful monitoring of temperature, pH levels, and fermentation times to achieve the desired outcome. Techniques such as cold fermentation, where vegetables are fermented at lower temperatures to slow down the process and develop deeper flavors, exemplify the meticulous approach needed. Similarly, recipes that involve stages of fermentation—such as fermenting garlic in honey before adding it to a vegetable ferment—require diligent attention to detail and timing. The success of these recipes hinges on the cook's ability to control and manipulate variables, ensuring that the final product achieves the intended flavor, texture, and safety standards.

The impact of advanced pickling and fermenting recipes on culinary traditions and contemporary cuisine is profound. These recipes bridge the past and present, drawing on ancient preservation methods while embracing modern culinary trends and innovations. They reflect the growing interest in artisanal foods and the desire for authentic, handcrafted experiences that connect eaters with the origins and transformations of their food. Advanced recipes also highlight the global nature of pickling and fermenting, incorporating ingredients and techniques from diverse culinary traditions to create something new and exciting. In this way, they contribute to the evolution of cuisine, challenging and expanding our understanding of what is possible in the world of food preservation.

Moreover, advanced pickling and fermenting recipes contribute to the sustainable food movement by promoting the use of seasonal, local produce and reducing food waste. Through fermentation and pickling, parts of fruits and vegetables that might otherwise be discarded—such as peels, cores, or wilted leaves—can be transformed into delicious, healthful additions to the diet. This approach not only maximizes the use of available resources but also encourages a more thoughtful and respectful relationship with food, emphasizing its value and the importance of minimizing waste.

In conclusion, advanced pickling and fermenting recipes represent the art and science of food preservation at its most sophisticated. They challenge cooks to explore complex flavor combinations, master precise techniques, and exercise patience and attention to detail. These recipes are a testament to the enduring appeal of fermented and pickled foods, bridging cultural traditions and contemporary culinary trends to create innovative and delicious dishes. As cooks continue experimenting with and refining these advanced techniques, they contribute to the rich tapestry of global cuisine, offering new tastes and textures that delight and inspire. In the hands of skilled practitioners, the ancient practices of pickling and fermenting continue to evolve, underscoring the limitless potential of these time-honored methods to enrich our culinary landscape.

CHAPTER VII

Practical Tips for Long-Term Food Preservation

Storing pickled and fermented foods

Storing pickled and fermented foods properly is crucial for maintaining their flavor, texture, safety, and nutritional value over time. These preservation methods have been used for centuries to lengthen the shelf life of foods that are perishable, allowing seasonal produce to be enjoyed throughout the year. However, the longevity and quality of pickled and fermented products depend significantly on the storage conditions they are kept in after the initial fermentation or pickling process is complete. This section explores the various aspects of storing pickled and fermented foods, including the importance of temperature control, container selection, and the role of pH levels, as well as providing insight into how these factors influence the safety and quality of preserved foods.

Temperature control is paramount when storing pickled and fermented foods. Most fermented foods thrive and continue to mature at specific temperatures, making it essential to store them in conditions that support their preservation and prevent spoilage. For most home fermentations, such as sauerkraut, kimchi, and fermented pickles, refrigeration at temperatures around 4°C (39°F) is ideal after the initial fermentation phase is complete. Refrigeration slows down the fermentation process, preserving the desired taste and texture of the product, and inhibits the growth of harmful bacteria. However, it's important to note that some fermented products, like certain types of aged cheeses and dry-cured meats, require specific humidity and temperature conditions that might differ from standard refrigeration.

The selection of appropriate containers for storing pickled and fermented foods is another crucial aspect of ensuring their longevity and quality. Glass jars with airtight lids are commonly used because they do not react with the acidity of the pickles or ferments, ensuring that the flavors remain unaltered. Furthermore, the transparency of glass allows for easy monitoring of the contents for any signs of spoilage, including mold growth or changes in texture. Plastic containers can also be used, provided they are food-grade and BPA-free to prevent chemical leaching. Regardless of the material, ensuring that containers are sterilized before use is essential to avoid contamination and spoilage.

Understanding and monitoring the pH levels of pickled and fermented foods are critical for storage. The acidity level, measured by the pH, is crucial in preserving these foods, as most harmful bacteria cannot survive in highly acidic environments. Most pickled and fermented foods should have a pH of 4.6 or lower, which not only contributes to their safety but also affects their taste and texture. Testing the pH of homemade pickles and ferments can be done with pH strips or meters, providing an extra layer of assurance about their safety for consumption. Storing foods at the correct pH levels ensures they stay safe to eat and retain their intended flavors over time.

Storing pickled and fermented foods properly also involves considerations of time. While these preservation methods significantly extend the shelf life of foods, they do not make them immortal. Over time, even adequately stored pickled and fermented foods can lose their crispness, flavor, or nutritional value. Being mindful of storage duration is essential; most pickled and fermented foods are best consumed within a few months to a year of being made, although some may keep longer under optimal conditions. Regularly checking stored foods for signs of spoilage, such as off-odors, changes in color, or the presence of mold, is crucial for ensuring their safety and quality.

In conclusion, storing pickled and fermented foods is a nuanced process that needs careful consideration of temperature, container choice, pH levels, and time. By adhering to best practices in storage, enthusiasts of pickling and fermenting can ensure that their culinary creations remain safe, delicious, and nutritious long after they have been made. Temperature control and the selection of appropriate, sterilized containers play crucial roles in maintaining the integrity of these foods. Monitoring pH levels adds an additional layer of safety, ensuring that the acidic environment needed to prevent spoilage is maintained. Finally, being mindful of storage duration and regularly inspecting stored foods for signs of spoilage are essential habits for anyone who wishes to enjoy the myriad benefits of pickled and fermented foods. With the proper storage techniques, the ancient arts of pickling and fermenting continue to offer modern cooks a reliable means of preserving the bounty of the harvest, exploring new flavors, and contributing to a healthful diet.

Rotation and inventory management

Effective rotation and inventory management are critical to maintaining a high-quality stock of pickled and fermented foods, whether for a home pantry, a commercial kitchen, or a small-scale production business. These practices ensure that products are used at their peak quality, reducing waste and maximizing these preserved foods' culinary and nutritional benefits. Pickled and fermented foods, with their extended shelf lives, present unique challenges and opportunities in inventory management. This section delves into strategies for successful rotation and inventory management, highlighting the importance of organization, tracking, and understanding the nuances of these preservation methods.

Organizing pickled and fermented foods begins with understanding their shelf life and storage conditions. While these foods are preserved and generally have a longer shelf life than their fresh counterparts, they can still deteriorate over time or when stored improperly. Establishing an organized storage system is crucial. This system could involve separating foods based on their type (e.g., pickles, kimchi, sauerkraut), storage method (refrigerated versus shelf-stable), or by date of production. Clear labeling of containers with the contents and the date of production or expiration date is essential for keeping track of what you have and ensuring that older items are used first. This "first in, first out" (FIFO) approach is a cornerstone of effective inventory management, reducing the risk of spoilage and ensuring that the oldest stock is used before newer batches.

Tracking inventory is another critical component of managing pickled and fermented foods. This can be as simple as maintaining a handwritten list or as sophisticated as using inventory management software. Tracking helps understand consumption patterns, particularly in commercial settings where predicting demand can inform production schedules. Home fermenters can aid in planning and ensuring a continuous supply of favorites without overproduction. Regular audits of the inventory, including physical checks, help identify any items that are nearing the end of their optimal consumption period, ensuring they are used promptly or, if necessary, disposed of safely.

Understanding the nuances of pickled and fermented foods is key to their rotation and inventory management. Unlike commercially processed foods, the shelf life of homemade ferments can vary widely depending on factors such as the ingredients used, the salt concentration, the fermentation time, and the storage conditions. For instance, sauerkraut fermented for a longer period may have a longer shelf life than a lightly fermented cucumber pickle. Recognizing these differences and adjusting rotation schedules accordingly can help maximize the inventory's quality and safety. It's also important to be vigilant for signs of spoilage, such as off-odors, mold growth, or changes in texture, which can occur even under ideal storage conditions.

Implementing rotation practices for pickled and fermented foods also involves educating those who access them, whether family members at home or staff in a commercial setting. Everyone should first know the importance of using older items and checking labels for production or expiration dates. In a commercial environment, training staff on proper handling and storage techniques is crucial to maintaining the quality and safety of the inventory. This education ensures that everyone contributes to the effective stock management, reducing waste and maintaining a high standard of food quality.

For businesses, especially those involved in selling pickled and fermented products, inventory management extends to predicting consumer demand and adjusting production accordingly. This requires a careful balance between maintaining enough stock to meet demand without overproducing, which can lead to waste. Seasonal variations in demand and trends in consumer preferences must be considered in production planning. Additionally, businesses must comply with food safety regulations, which may dictate specific practices in picking, storing, and rotating pickled and fermented foods.

In conclusion, effective rotation and inventory management of pickled and fermented foods are essential practices that ensure these products' quality, safety, and enjoyment. Organizing the inventory clearly, tracking stock levels, understanding the unique characteristics of different ferments, educating those involved in their use, and adjusting production based on demand are all critical components of successful management. Whether managing a home pantry filled with jars of homemade pickles and sauerkraut or overseeing a commercial operation producing artisanal fermented products, attention to detail in rotation and inventory management can significantly enhance the overall experience of enjoying these age-old preservation methods. By embracing these practices, enthusiasts and professionals alike can ensure that their pickled and fermented foods are consumed at their peak, reducing waste and celebrating the rich flavors and health benefits these foods offer.

Incorporating pickled and fermented foods into everyday meals

Incorporating pickled and fermented foods into everyday meals is not just a trend but a return to ancient dietary practices that have sustained cultures around the globe. These foods offer a unique combination of flavors, textures, and health benefits that can enhance daily meals' nutritional value and taste. From the tangy crunch of sauerkraut to the spicy depth of kimchi, and the sharp zest of pickled cucumbers, fermented foods bring diversity to the table that can invigorate the routine of everyday eating. This section explores the benefits of including pickled and fermented foods in daily diets, offering practical tips on seamlessly integrating these foods into various meals, thereby broadening culinary horizons while bolstering health.

The nutritional benefits of pickled and fermented foods are well-documented. These foods are rich in probiotics, the helpful bacteria that are crucial in gut health. A healthy gut microbiome is interconnected to improved digestion, enhanced immune function, and a minimized risk of many chronic diseases. Additionally, the fermentation process can expand the bioavailability of nutrients, making specific vitamins and minerals more accessible to the body. Moreover, fermented foods are often low in calories yet high in flavor, making them an excellent addition to diets for those looking to maintain or lose weight without sacrificing taste.

Integrating pickled and fermented foods into breakfast can be a refreshing way to start the day. A dollop of kimchi or sauerkraut can add a flavorful and probiotic boost to scrambled eggs or omelets. Yogurt, a fermented dairy product, is a perfect base for fruit and granola, while kefir, a drinkable yogurt, can be blended into smoothies for a tangy twist. For those who enjoy savory breakfasts, pickled vegetables can be a great addition to avocado toast, contrasting flavors and textures that wake up the palate.

Lunch offers another opportunity to incorporate these foods into the diet. Fermented foods can add interest and nutrition to salads; for example, pickled beets or carrots can lend a sweet and tangy flavor to leafy greens, while a spoonful of miso—a fermented soybean paste—can elevate a simple vinaigrette dressing. Sandwiches and wraps can also benefit from the inclusion of pickled cucumbers, onions, or peppers, offering a crunchy, flavorful element that complements a variety of fillings from cold cuts to grilled vegetables.

Dinner time presents a broad canvas for creatively using pickled and fermented foods. These ingredients can serve as condiments, enhance the main dishes' flavors, or be incorporated directly into recipes. For instance, chopped kimchi can be stirred into fried rice or noodle dishes, imparting a spicy complexity that enriches the meal. Fermented foods can also be used as a base for sauces and marinades; yogurt can tenderize meats while adding a subtle tanginess. Additionally, pickled vegetables can accompany grilled meats or fish as a side dish, offering a refreshing counterpoint to rich flavors.

Snacks and sides are perhaps the easiest categories for integrating pickled and fermented foods into everyday eating. A quick snack of pickled cucumbers, green beans, or cauliflower can satisfy crunchy cravings without the empty calories of processed snacks. Fermented foods like kimchi or sauerkraut can be served as simple sides with lunch or dinner, providing a probiotic boost with minimal effort. Even desserts can benefit from adding fermented ingredients; for example, yogurt can be used in baking to add moisture as well as a slight tang to cakes and bread.

Lastly, embracing creativity is vital to successfully incorporating pickled and fermented foods into daily meals. Experimenting with various flavor combinations and textures can produce new culinary discoveries and prevent mealtime monotony. Mixing and matching these foods with familiar ingredients can also ease the transition for those who may be new to the flavors of fermentation, gradually introducing them to the diverse world of pickled and fermented delicacies.

In conclusion, incorporating pickled and fermented foods into everyday meals offers many benefits, from enhanced flavor profiles and added nutritional value to improved gut health. With their rich history and diverse culinary applications, these foods can transform ordinary meals into extraordinary experiences. By starting with small additions to breakfast, lunch, dinner, and snacks, individuals can gradually explore the vast potential of fermented foods, discovering new favorites and reaping the health benefits along the way. With a little creativity and openness to experimentation, integrating pickled and fermented foods into daily diets can become a practice and a pleasure, enriching the culinary landscape of everyday eating.

Safety precautions for long-term storage

The long-term storage of pickled and fermented foods is a practice rooted in ancient traditions, serving as a cornerstone for preserving the bounty of harvests and enhancing flavors through the slow alchemy of fermentation. This process extends the shelf life of perishable items and enriches foods with complex flavors and probiotic benefits. However, ensuring the safety of these preserved foods over extended periods requires careful attention to specific precautions. This section explores the critical safety measures necessary for the long-term storage of pickled and fermented foods, emphasizing the importance of cleanliness, proper storage conditions, pH monitoring, container selection, and awareness of spoilage signs.

Cleanliness is paramount in the preparation and storage of pickled and fermented foods. The initial step in ensuring safety is sterilizing all equipment, containers, and utensils used in pickling or fermenting. This includes jars, lids, cutting boards, knives, and even the fermenter's hands. Bacteria, yeasts, and molds are ever- present in the environment, and while some are beneficial for fermentation, others can spoil food and pose health risks. By thoroughly cleaning and sterilizing all equipment, the risk of introducing harmful pathogens is significantly minimized, creating a safe environment for the desired fermentation processes to occur.

Proper storage conditions are essential for keeping the safety and quality of pickled and fermented foods during long-term storage. Most fermented foods require refrigeration once the active fermentation phase is complete to slow microbial activity and prevent spoilage. The ideal refrigerator temperature for storing these foods is between zero °C to four °C (32°F to 39°F). A cool, dark pantry or cellar may suffice for pickled foods stored in vinegar or brine without active fermentation, provided the temperature remains consistent and not prone to fluctuations that could encourage spoilage.

Monitoring the pH level of pickled and fermented foods is a vital safety measure. The acidity in these foods inhibits the growth of harmful bacteria, with a pH of 4.6 or lower being generally recognized as safe. It's advisable to use pH strips or a digital pH meter to check the acidity level, especially in home-prepared pickles and ferments. Ensuring the pH is within the safe range before and during storage is essential for preventing the growth of pathogens, including botulism-causing bacteria, which can thrive in low-acid, anaerobic environments.

The selection of appropriate containers also plays a significant role in the safety of storing pickled and fermented foods. Non-reactive containers which includes glass or food-grade plastic are ideal, as they do not interact with acidic foods in a way that could leach harmful substances into the food or degrade the container itself. Metal containers should be avoided except those specifically designed for acidic foods. Furthermore, ensuring airtight seals on containers helps maintain an anaerobic environment crucial for fermented foods and prevents contamination from outside sources.

Being vigilant for signs of spoilage is an ongoing aspect of safely storing pickled and fermented foods. Indicators such as mold growth, off-odors, gas bubbles in jars that should be inactive, and changes in texture or color can all signal that the food has become unsafe to eat. Regularly inspecting stored foods allows for early detection of spoilage, preventing the consumption of compromised foods. If any doubt arises about the safety of a pickled or fermented item, it is best to err on the side of caution and discard it.

In conclusion, the long-term storage of pickled and fermented foods, while rooted in ancient practices, demands modern understanding and diligence to ensure safety. By adhering to stringent cleanliness protocols, maintaining proper storage conditions, monitoring acidity levels, selecting appropriate containers, and being vigilant for spoilage, enthusiasts of pickling and fermenting can safely enjoy the fruits of their labor for months or even years. These precautions safeguard health and preserve the quality and integrity of these cherished culinary traditions. As interest in home pickling and fermenting grows, so does the importance of implementing these safety measures, ensuring that the art of preservation remains both a joy and a benefit to all who partake.

CONCLUSION

In conclusion, "Pickling and Fermenting Recipes for Survival: Delicious Dishes for the Long Haul" stands as a comprehensive guide to the timeless arts of pickling and fermenting, offering readers a wealth of knowledge, inspiration, and practical guidance. Throughout the pages of this book, we have explored the myriad benefits of pickling and fermenting for survival, from their ability to extend the shelf life of perishable foods to their capacity to preserve nutrients, flavor, and cultural heritage.

As we navigate an increasingly uncertain world marked by environmental volatility, economic instability, and global disruptions to food supply chains, the importance of pickling and fermenting for survival has never been more apparent. In times of plenty, these age-old techniques enable individuals to make the most of seasonal harvests, capturing the vibrancy of fresh produce in jars and crocks to enjoy throughout the year. In times of scarcity, they provide a lifeline, ensuring access to nourishing and flavorful provisions that can sustain us through lean periods and emergencies.

Moreover, pickling and fermenting offer a means of fostering resilience, empowerment, and connection—to our food, our communities, and our ancestors' wisdom. By embracing these time-honored practices, individuals can cultivate self-reliance, reduce food waste, and honor the cultural traditions that have sustained communities for centuries. Whether through the tangy crunch of pickled cucumbers, the fiery kick of fermented hot sauce, or the complex umami notes of kimchi, pickling and fermenting invite us to explore the rich tapestry of flavors and ingredients that make up our culinary heritage.

Throughout this book, readers have been introduced to diverse recipes, techniques, and tips designed to empower them on their journey toward self-sufficiency and abundance. From the basics of pickling and fermenting to advanced methods and troubleshooting tips, every aspect of the process has been carefully considered to ensure success and satisfaction in the kitchen. Whether you're a novice fermenter or a seasoned practitioner, there's something for everyone within these pages—a wealth of inspiration to spark your creativity and fuel your culinary adventures.

As we embark on this journey together, may "Pickling and Fermenting Recipes for Survival" serve as a beacon of hope and empowerment, guiding readers toward a future where self-reliance and abundance go hand in hand. By embracing the age-old art of pickling and fermenting, we can nourish our bodies, cultivate resilience, and forge connections to the past that will sustain us through whatever challenges. In the face of uncertainty, pickling and fermenting offer sustenance and a taste of the enduring wisdom of the ages—a reminder that in times of hardship, the power to thrive lies within our hands and hearts.

www.ingramcontent.com/pod-product-compliance
Lightning Source LLC
Chambersburg PA
CBHW072011150726
47999CB00002B/598